*The Art of Getting
Your Own Sweet Way*

The Art of Getting Your Own Sweet Way

PHILIP B. CROSBY

McGRAW-HILL BOOK COMPANY
New York   St. Louis   San Francisco   Düsseldorf   Johannesburg
Kuala Lumpur   London   Mexico   Montreal   New Delhi   Panama
Rio de Janeiro   Singapore   Sydney   Toronto

Library of Congress Cataloging in Publication Data

Crosby, Philip B.
  The art of getting your own sweet way.

  1. Management. 2. Success. I. Title.
HD 38.C68   658.4   71-177371
ISBN 0-07-014510-5

1234567890 BPBP 765432

This book was set in Linofilm Baskerville by Vail-Ballou
Press, Inc., and printed and bound by The Book Press.
The editors were W. Hodson Morgan and Lydia
Maiorca. The designer was Naomi Auerbach. Teresa F.
Leaden supervised production.

To Philip and Phylis—who manage

Contents

Preface

*T*he test of a Situation Manager is this: Can you continually arrange your personal world so that you can do what you want to do and have everyone else happy that things are turning out so well for you?

This may sound like the definition of a spoiled brat, for certainly this is what they achieve. The difference is that people don't really like or admire a spoiled brat. Situation Managers they like, because he arranges it to be so.

I hope that you have an uncontrollable urge to accomplish this environment for yourself, because if you do, you will read this relatively short book carefully.

Let me give you an example. I had the problem of finding the leaders within a specific functional operation scattered all about the world. There were 300 men serving as managers of this discipline. After mulling it over for some time, I sent each of them a personal invitation to come to a meeting in New York. I purposely did not write the invitation on my official stationery, and I did not mention the meeting to the top management executives who could have lent it an air of authority. Twenty-one of the men showed up. They were the ones who had control of their top management. They were the thought leaders. Five years of experi ence with the whole 300 did not show any new ones.

If you ask a typical manager his biggest problem, he will tell you that his boss doesn't understand. A husband will say his wife doesn't understand, and so on into the next generation. Situation Managers make sure everyone understands. They do this by explaining things in terms that are dear to the hearts of the understandee.

I am a nontechnical man in a technical world. Technical things don't interest me, except in their abstract form. There were times when I used to have to keep a translator around to explain to me what my engineers were saying. It was almost like the western movies where the scout would turn to the cavalry officer and start: "Him say . . ."

It occurred to me some years ago that problems, whether technically oriented or not, do not exist until they are identified and described by a person. Since the person doing so invariably tilts his description of the problem to suit his own ends or bias, the important thing was to know how to get the real story out of the participants. Once you know the real story, the solution is easy.

I really believe that all the big wars were caused only because the key people didn't understand the situation. And once committed, they couldn't find a graceful way out. Therefore, all of us suffered. Our own Civil War was essentially a bluffing contest for the first 18 months or so until the whole thing got out of hand. The card holders suddenly found that the situation had been snatched from them by events. The battles seem to have very little to do with the outcome of the war.

The only honest wars ever fought were those between small, politically independent units such as tribes, duchies, and the like. There the motive was quite clear: greed. When one tribe fought another, it was to grab something the other one had. Nations get the whole thing complicated around honor, freedom, and other titles that mean different things to different people. Greed you can understand and appreciate.

We as individuals fight an unending number of personal wars. It may be against something as impressive as the Power Structure, or it may just be combat with a sales clerk. At any rate, we are constantly being tried and found either wanting or not wanting. As you build a reputation for being able to handle whatever comes along, you get tried less.

Each of us performs as individuals, and we have the opportunity to have war or peace within our own world as we wish. How well we anticipate problems and how well we handle those that exist are all that matters. Those who handle problems well prosper. Those who don't find excuses.

The thought patterns for Situation Analysis and Situation Prevention contained herein have been worked out carefully through trial and error. Any inadequacies you may find in them are my own fault, and no one else's. I believe they work because I use them every day. I'd be interested to know how you get along with them.

The book has been set up to bear heavily on real-life situations as a base for examining these thought-taking guides. If you recognize anyone you know in any of these situations, please don't tell him. As far as I can tell, no real persons were used as any part of these stories. They are entirely fictional.

I would like to express my gratitude to my wife, Shirley, who besides having to put up with a lot of discomfort when I started writing, has had the patience to read the results one word at a time and gently point out, to my disbelieving ears, the illogical and misleading. Whatever I accomplish in the world will be due to her support, understanding, and love. Also, like the Tamarack CC golf course, and the New Haven RR, she keeps me humble.

I owe a vote of thanks to Louie, the conciérge of the Westbury-Brussels who keeps for me what used to be my typewriter and is now "our machine."

It is customary to end a preface by stating that there are a lot of people to whom the author owes thanks but that there is not enough room to mention them. I'd like to change that rule here and list some of those people I have met through the years who, in my opinion, can qualify as senior Situation Managers. If there is ever a society of Situation Managers, these should be the charter members. They always seem to get their own way.

H. A. C. Anderson, Rich Bennett, Bud Blandford, Georges Borel, Peggy Cox, Virginia Creed, David Crosby, John De-Lorean, Dick Dertinger, Tim Dunleavy, Carl Foster, Frankie Franklyn, Harold Geneen, Ned Gerrity, Jim Halpin, Harry Hamm, Jack Hanway, Russ Hulbert, Virginia Knauer, Herb Knortz, Dave and Joe Lefferman, Jim Lester, Ed Monk, Bud Morrow, Ed Schaffer, Dick Silver, Sam Snead, Herman Staudt, Maury Valente, Bob Vincent, Werner Von Braun, G. T. Willey, Ray Woody.

Obviously I have left out a lot of people. I have only included those whom I have personally seen in action.

This book is dedicated to, and is the property of, my children Philip and Phylis. They know how it is done.

Phil Crosby

The Concept of Situation Management

People are raised to believe that things just happen to them and there isn't much they can do about it. Therefore, they concentrate on a specific field in order to earn a living and provide a purpose in their existence. When situations arise outside of this specific field, they feel a lack of expertise and just handle things as best they can. Usually their result is to lose a little ground each time. It is such results that develop the cynicism of age.

However, it doesn't have to be like that. The management of situations can be handled quite easily by anyone of average capability who is willing to follow a logical thought pattern. This pattern is not difficult to learn and can be rehearsed to perfection by application within the person's acknowledged field of competence. The resulting successes supply a confidence factor.

Situations only involve people, and people are not really very complicated concerning their wants and actions. They just want to get their own sweet way.

The Situation Manager can get his own way and have other people want it to happen, if he remains calm and un-emotional while following his logical program.

*The Art of Getting
Your Own Sweet Way*

Introduction to
Situation Management

You nave probably noticed that the world was not designed specifically for you.

Each day we must attend to the struggle of adjusting ourselves to the world, or the world to ourselves. This is not necessarily an unenjoyable process. Life can be happy, purposeful, and pleasant. The only requirement is that we successfully resolve the continuous situations presented to us by our social, business, political, family, and physical environments.

The success average we maintain in this activity determines the amount of happiness, purposefulness, and pleasantness we will enjoy. Thus Situation Management, and the strategy for employing it is a vital tool.

We all manage for a living, whether it be getting a

1

husband out the door in the morning or manipulating an international financial deal.

Because of this, the Situation Manager must develop a logical, repeatable method of resolving each difficulty he faces and at the same time adjust the whole event to his advantage. He must also learn how to prevent the situation from happening to him in the first place.

Prevention is more difficult. Extraction from situations by one means or another is somewhat instinctive. That is because it is "now." But prevention is a future thing, and if we are to prevent, we must recognize the potential for a difficult situation to occur. This is difficult since it requires accepting an awareness of vulnerability that is contrary to the inborn conspiracy of immortality each of us carries. Therefore, the approach must be systematic and disciplinary, or we won't do it.

What are situations?

They are occurrences which cause people to be faced with action decisions in order to return their life to its status prior to the occurrence. The action decisions they make, and the actions they take, determine whether the eventual result will increase or decrease their personal satisfaction with life.

Opportunities for success are situations, so are opportunities for failure. While the overwhelming majority of situations can be understood and handled by people who are willing to give it proper thought, some cannot. Someone falling overboard in the middle of the night might be stumped for an effective action as the ship sails out of sight and sharks move closer.

However, those faced with a misinformed boss, an irate wife, an unlockable suitcase, or a broken promise know that it will be solved somehow. Their concern is to have it resolved in their favor, regularly.

To learn how to accomplish this, we must delve into the intricacies of Situation Management.

The problem we face in becoming effective Situation Managers is the same challenge presented in all aspects of our daily life: How do we learn quickly enough by experience and education to handle all possible situations?

The housewife, postman, computer programmer, bus driver, machinist, secretary, executive, builder, banker, soldier, taxi driver, stockbroker, engineer, husband, pilot, administrator, scientist, plumber, lodge chairman, elder, minister, Democrat, Republican, fisherman, golfer, father, mother, sister, brother, aunt, uncle, politician, etc., must learn to handle situations caused by other housewives, postmen, computer programmers, bus drivers, and on and on.

The difficulty comes from two basic causes:

1. None of us is only one thing. We are a combination of many occupations, responsibilities, and desires.

2. Most adverse situations are, at least in part, created by ourselves.

Because of these two characteristics, we tend to view each situation defensively and usually concentrate our first efforts toward showing that we are indeed innocent victims of the inefficiencies or malevolences of others.

Consider:

1. You double-park for two minutes in front of the cleaners and rushingly return to find a $15 ticket on your car. You note that adequate parking has not been provided, that you had no other choice, and that obvious traffic violations are being committed all around you. You are upset that you have been thus picked upon.

2. You go to your favorite restaurant with an important guest. The maitre d' greets you by name but confesses that without a reservation he cannot place you. Yet there are tables open as you can plainly see. You are hurt at their ingratitude and embarrassed by the necessity to seek another place. It seems that they should take better care of their old customers.

3. The production department promised you that they

would deliver some equipment by the end of the month, and you have given the customer your word on it. Then you find out that the stuff wasn't shipped. You berate production, and they tell you that there was a good reason. You know that there can't be a good reason. Why did they let you down?

4. You are driving along a deserted road late at night. Suddenly you have a blowout. The spare turns out to be flat also. As you stumble 3 miles through the dark, you rehearse a speech to your service station manager. Why is he so irresponsible?

These are all situations that can happen or have happened to each of us. Our reaction is typical and predictable. The real question involved seems to be one concerning the "rights of man." Certainly a noble and profound subject. Extensive discussion of that particular point in any of these situations would produce a complete standoff and quite possibly a revolution. Revolutions, or their encouragement, are avoided in management situations because they seem to reproduce the exact situation that existed prior to upheaval. This merely postpones resolution of the situation.

What we are concerned with here are two aspects: (1) how to extract ourselves from the present condition we find ourselves facing, and (2) how to prevent such situations from engulfing us by never getting into them in the first place.

Let's apply those thoughts to the situations described:

Number 1 Extraction: Pay the $15 and send the receipt to the cleaner with a suggestion that he provide adequate parking or enter into a free delivery service. He may repay you. But remember that you parked the car, not he.

PREVENTION: Select cleaners that have adequate parking in the first place.

Number 2 Extraction: Slip the maitre d' $5, while being gracious about it, and humbly state that you'll remember to make a reservation next time. Whether you go back there again is a different thing, but it is better not to expose your inadequacies to the customer.

PREVENTION: When you make the luncheon appointment, routinely make a reservation. You've known that is the way they operate. Or else resign yourself to adding $5 to the lunch bill each time.

Number 3 Extraction: Let the production people tell you the reason. It might be that the customer wanted a last minute change, that the plant went on strike, or even that the product didn't work. If the reason is good enough to let them break their promise to you, it is probably good enough for you to use on the customer. If it isn't good enough, then take the production manager with you while you explain. He'll learn a good lesson and the customer will be flattered at the attention.

PREVENTION: People who make promises based on secondhand information deserve what happens to them. You gave your word quite casually. You should have looked at their plans and schedules first in order to assure yourself that they had adequate time to handle any disasters that might occur.

Number 4 Extraction: You can drive along with a flat tire as quickly as you can walk. If you go slowly enough, the tire will last for 10 or 15 miles and you'll at least have light and shelter. If nothing else, stay in the car. If nobody comes along during the night, you'll at least have a fighting chance when the sun comes up. Don't make the situation worse.

PREVENTION: How did that flat tire get in there? Make sure you weren't the bad guy. How did the tires get worn enough to blow out? A flat can happen to anyone, but blowouts come from old and worn tires. No one interested in preventing dangerous situations can afford worn out equipment.

If these discussions do not seem particularly earthshaking to you, you might try other everyday examples, like: "How did a nice girl like you get into a business like this?" or "How do I keep from getting soap in my eyes?"

We exist in situations. We manage situations. We are managed by situations. All we need to do in order to control our life is to detect, understand, and resolve situations. Managers spend all day and most of the night working on their problems. Problems are their life's blood. However, very few take the time to understand the meat of their problems. That is the difference between the managers who work their little hearts out and accomplish nothing and those who are truly effective yet appear unconcerned. The logic of Situation Management can let you join the corps of the latter.

Consider what these overworked managers do. They read reports. They write reports. Reading has its own speed, and there are methods for increasing it that every manager knows. Those who spend their time going to speed-reading school receive their own rewards. But how about the matter of writing reports? Did you ever see someone burn the midnight oil to write a report? Certainly you did. Perhaps you have done it yourself. Why does it require so much shuffling of paper, scratching of head, and correction of drafts? Only because they don't understand the situation. Who can write about something that is not clear to him? Why spend so much time on execution and so little on comprehension?

If you truly understand the concept of Situation Management, you will be able to reduce your personal effort to a minimum. You will then have time to arrange your own situations and sit happily, while others struggle to read and report. You can even be your own man.

The only manager this method will help is the one who conscientiously applies Situation Management to the skills he already has. Obvious? Not necessarily. There are those who search for the easy solution, but as you know there are no easy solutions—there are only consistent philosophies. Consistency wins, whether it wants to or not.

Situation Management won't make you a super-manager unless you know your business. But you can know your business and still be a minor-manager, unless you consider controlling instead of being.

There are only two kinds of managers: the growing and the obsolete. Unfortunately the obsolete managers never recognize that they have reached this stage, although it is obvious to everyone else. The obsolete manager has had all the experiences available and has a drawer full of available solutions, or at least he thinks he has.

As you become more involved in the stories described in the following chapters, you should start consciously applying the practices to your own problems. Start with little ones first and work up.

Situation Management is not like a tug of war. It matters not how many people are on each side. Your team will always consist of one member. You have no organization to worry about, no problems of requiring concensus on strategy, and no reports to submit. It is you, determined, fit, and resolved, on one side—the world on the other. That way, you can want your thing to happen more than they don't want it to happen.

Let's review the Laws of Situation Management first, since they provide an understanding of what causes situations to occur and they give you an insight into the way people are going to react.

Then we'll explore the process of situation analysis by resolving real-life situations, explaining each phase as it occurs. After that, we can review situation prevention.

Set your mind on open, and let's begin.

Crosby's Laws of Situation Management

Since the purpose of this book is to prepare us to face a world dedicated to advancing further and faster than we can automatically comprehend, it follows that we should prepare ourselves to handle it methodically. The material aspects of the world may and do change. But people are pretty much the same as far as their personal concerns and motivations. Their basic actions in situations relate to the Laws of Situation Management.

These laws are really guidelines. They exist to help you categorize the reasons people do the things they do and to provide guidance on the aspects of social intercourse that are important to Situation Managers.

If you study the laws carefully and don't fall victim to Law No. 10, you will be in good shape to handle the

Situation Analysis and Prevention activities described in the following chapters.

People are not complex. They really just want to achieve their personal definition of peace and quiet and to have their own sweet way. They don't really mean most of the things they say but will die rather than admit it. Their behavior patterns are as repetitious as their conversations. But people are what make the world go 'round, and we must learn to deal with them.

CROSBY'S LAWS
OF SITUATION MANAGEMENT

1. The primary concern of management is survival.
2. A person's loyalty is a function of how much he feels he is appreciated.
3. The amount of accurate information an executive possesses concerning the status of his operation varies inversely with his position in the organization.
4. The effectiveness of any program depends upon the amount of participation delegated.
5. The less systematic support a decision maker receives, the better decisions he will make.
6. Pride goes before all.
7. A job can only be as successful as the means supplied to measure it.
8. People are more important to situations than things.
9. Improvement is the only practical management goal.
10. Nobody really listens.

LAW NO. 1
The primary concern of management
is survival.

All managers are scared to death that they are going to fail. They know the only way not to fail is to remain in command.

This occurs because they, like the rest of us, are basically insecure. Here they are in charge of something, and they don't know everything there is to know about it. No matter how firmly they speak or how positively they act, they really believe this, probably because it is true. Therefore, some play a constant game of being up on the other fellow by constantly trying to keep him off balance. Their own personal well-being and security is at the root of all their actions.

The Situation Manager must recognize this and consider it in all interactions with management people.

There may be those who think this to be a law developed through cynicism. Actually it comes about the other way. It is a message of hope. Managers can view their own Situation Management activities clearly when the test is: "Will I survive this action?" After all, if the management survives, the operation will survive. There is only management so long as there is something to manage. This thought applies to nations, companies, marriages, colleges, or other legally constructed enterprises. Walk up to any department head in your company and say: "I understand that the board is going to petition to put the company into receivership." He will reply: "How do you feel that will affect my department?"

Approach your young son and state: "We are moving to South Africa tomorrow." He will say: "Will I have my own room?"

Tell your Protestant minister: "I understand that the pope is visiting us next Sunday." He will say: "Do you think the church looks clean enough?"

All that really matters to managers is self and the survival of that self. I am sure that many of us would turn ourselves out into the jungle and submit to a life of meditation, herbs, and loneliness if it could be proved beyond the shadow of a doubt that this would benefit the world. Because it cannot be so proved, we must fight on to preserve that which makes us secure, since that is what will improve the world as we see it.

Survival depends upon controlling your environment. Survival is always providing the image of achievement and, at the same time, avoiding nonpurposeful conflict. Those who would muddle your world must be identified, analyzed, and disposed of quickly and cleanly. Violence is neither permitted nor encouraged, not only because violence is nasty but because it is not nearly so much fun as Situation Management.

A management's proposals to its stockholders must be couched in such a way that denial or modification of a specific proposal would not destroy the management. (Remember De Gaulle.) You cannot put your plans into effect if you are not there. If your whole program rests on a single yes or no, then you have little better than a 50-50 survival opportunity. You must provide alternatives that are equally acceptable to you because they achieve the same end, or else you will find yourself defending unto death something that is really not important. For instance:

You don't say: "The place must be painted now."

You say: "I suggest starting our maintenance program with the paint task."

You don't say: "We must attack Zubania before they can hit us."

You say: "Our defense plan must take into consideration the discovery of an intended enemy offensive."

You don't say: "Our new programs will require an immediate tax increase of 25 percent, and it must start as soon as possible."

You say: "The people really want these new programs. Let us select the several ways of paying for them and submit them to a vote."

You don't say: "The most important thing to me is money and if I don't get more, I'm going to quit."

You say: "One of the ways our company is measured by stock analysts, customers, and the public is the amount of money we pay our key executives. They expect important people to make important money."

When you approach a situation that needs to be managed or prevented, you must remember it is the final score that counts, not just form. While this score requires the keeping of

integrity and morals, it does not necessarily require the assuming of scars and wounds. If something is inevitable, like a
merger, it is better to recognize the inevitability and utilize it
to your advantage. The history of mergers in a free enterprise
community usually is that the company absorbed fights the
controls and suggestions of the new mother company to the
extent that after a year, or so, their original organization and
management is impossible to find. Some have been removed.
Some left in a fit of pique. Some have just disappeared into
the barely visible mist of "lower-middle management." (Lower-middle management is three levels below wherever you happen to be at the moment.) These tragedies occur for the most
part because the individuals involved assume an erroneous
and false pride that requires them to reject every suggestion,
technique, or approach offered by the absorbing operation.
They forget that the representatives coming to visit them are
just as nervous about the situation as they are.

To make sure that your management ideals are the eventual winners, you must accept the proffered controls, suggestions, and inspirations in a manner that creates confidence and
trust. You must become part of the crusade—the good gray
judge who always looks at both sides. One of these days they
will move you into their tent, and you will have your opportunity to turn things around to the way you prefer them. If you
do not survive, the opportunity will not happen. Consider the
Mamelukes.

Instead of waiting for an audit or evaluation, request one.
Then you can schedule it and probably even run the meeting.
Don't be defensive, be positive. Some of their recommendations are bound to be good. But as you cheer them on, don't
forget to price each suggestion. When the proper time comes,
you can present the bill for all the improvements. If you get
the money, you're way ahead. If you don't get it, no one can
fault you. Perhaps the items were not made clear enough. Ask
for another audit. Your stature will rise, the audits will continue, and nothing will change unless you wish it.

Wives have been using this technique for years. They don't have to think it out. Some sort of Holy Spirit bestows it upon them immediately after the husband says: "I do." See if some of these remarks are familiar.

"I think it is wonderful the way you continue to work for Mr. Girbley, although you are smarter than he is. Even if that new offer does pay more money and we could live a little more comfortably, I wouldn't want you to let that poor old man down. He'll probably recognize your talents someday."

"Do you want to eat dinner before or after we visit my mother tonight?"

"I can't seem to make our budget come out the way you explained it to me. Could you go over it again? One point I'm particularly confused about is in what category I should place your new golf clubs."

"Your son hit the boy across the street today."

If you notice the swing of these statements, it is apparent that the husband has somehow become the ogre who is doing in the innocents. Protest or clarification has already been written off. There are no effective answers except male rage or petulance which can be handled as if it didn't exist. The *superior* has been reminded of his proper place in the scheme of things.

Let us return to the matter of the merger.

Big Daddy, Inc., an acquiring-type company, has purchased Outgo from its owners, the Outgoing family. While the family is in the counting house leafing through their new shares of Big Daddy certificates, the professional management of Outgo is suffering some concern. The several key managers have gathered in the office of Outgo president Harold Hardwood to question their future. After all, the pay is good, and the work is not too hard. Who knows what will happen when Big Daddy comes in?

"Gentlemen," soothes Mr. Hardwood, "please calm down. We will resolve this situation to our advantage, but you are all going to have to follow four rules: First, in our dealings with our brothers from Big Daddy, you must be open in all relationships and answer truthfully every question they ask you. Second, it is not necessary to volunteer information because if they wanted to know that particular thing, they would have asked you.

"Third, always say 'we' when speaking of the merger. Don't say 'you' or 'us.' Fourth, if someone provides you with a truly useful bit of information or guidance, be grateful. If they are impractical, smile a lot. That is all you have to do. Leave the rest to me."

When A. C. Bustle, the Big Daddy group executive, and his staff of four arrived at Outgo, they were met at the airplane by Mr. Hardwood himself. Hardwood insisted on carrying A. C.'s suitcase to the old company station wagon and, puffing only slightly, drove the executives toward the Outgo plant. As they exchanged casual conversation during the drive, Bustle noted that the wagon had obviously been used to carry machinery and there was quite a bit of grease splattered about the back seat. Two of his men were attempting to wipe grease spots off their suits. "Don't worry about the grease," smiled Hardwood, "we'll get that off quick as a jiffy when we get back to the plant. We have some fluid that cuts the stuff like nothing."

"This seems to be a multipurposed car you have here," said Bustle.

"Only one we have," replied Hardwood. "Have to keep ex penses down. I'm sure you fellows at Big Daddy feel like that too. Don't you?"

"Certainly we do, Mr. Hardwood. May I call you Harold? Yes, we are very concerned about expenses, Harold, but we also like to preserve a little of our image. We probably ought to get a less messy form of transportation."

"I'm glad to hear you say that, A. C.," said Hardwood. "The Outgoing family was so tight that I thought we'd never be able to get a decent automobile. I'll take care of that right away." He drove off into a dirt road muttering something about a "shortcut" and it became too noisy for conversation.

The atmosphere at Outgo was the most friendly Bustle and his team had ever encountered. The fluid really did clean the spots off the clothes, and they all sat down to a plain but well-prepared lunch in the small executive dining room of the plant. The Outgo key executives had joined the group, and the Big Daddy team soon found themselves explaining all about the mother company, its plans, and its people to an interested and attentive audience. Every now and then an Outgo executive would ask a question to clarify a point, and then jot the answer down in a note pad.

After a tour of the plant, the staff specialists met with their counterparts, while Bustle and Hardwood went over the general status of the operation.

Bustle was genuinely pleased at the progress he and Hardwood were making, until they reached the area of purchasing. Bustle noted that it was Outgo's practice to pay expediting fees on practically every piece of material received. "We have done that for the purpose of keeping our inventory low. There really isn't much room here in this facility to store things; so we've just always done it this way."

"That is the problem with a lot of management today, Harold," philosophized Bustle. "We do many things because we've always done it that way. In this case, it would probably be less expensive in the long run to build a warehouse and place large orders at discount prices."

"I'll look into that right away, A. C.," said Hardwood, making a note.

That evening the Outgo staff hosted the Big Daddy visitors at the country club to introduce them to the rest of their team. Bustle pulled Hardwood aside after dinner and complimented him on the arrangements and the attitudes of his people.

"However, Harold, I should say that this party, however

well intended, is probably too expensive for what it will accomplish. You must always look at the return you will get for what you invest."

Hardwood thought about this for a moment. "I see what you mean, A. C.. You sure know how to put your finger on the meat of the problem. I imagine you feel we should do something about our executive dining room at the plant, too."

"Well," smiled A. C., "I hadn't planned to mention it this trip, but now that you brought it up, I do feel that it might be better to have the dining room catered rather than to have a permanent staff on hand to prepare the meals. Food would probably be just as good, and I'm sure it would be less expensive. If nothing else, we would save the fringe benefits we are now paying those employees."

"Good point," nodded Hardwood. "I'll take care of it immediately."

The next morning the Big Daddy team presented its full report concerning the evaluation they had made of Outgo. Hardwood had made careful notation of each point and stated after the meeting that he really appreciated the concern and wisdom expressed by the visitors. He promised a full action report within 2 weeks. The team was driven back to the airport in the same station wagon, but this time the inside was covered with bed sheets in order to protect their clothes.

Three weeks later, A. C. Bustle was called to the office of the Big Daddy president. "A. C., I have just received the action report from Outgo. They moved on every item your team presented to them, and there is a note from Hardwood taking special pains to point out that he personally appreciated the help and guidance you had given him. A fine job, Bustle. In fact, I'd like to drop down there and see the place. This fellow Hardwood sounds like a very cooperative person."

When the Big Daddy president arrived to visit Outgo, he was driven to the plant in a new Cadillac. The ride was very pleasant, including no shortcuts, and the president found himself concerned with only one minor item: the seats of the car were covered with bed sheets. "To keep you from getting oil on your clothes," explained the driver.

Harold Hardwood greeted the president at the front door and immediately conducted him, along with his group, on a brief but informative tour of the plant. As they went through each department, Hardwood pointed out improvements that had been suggested by the Big Daddy team on its previous visit. He invited the department supervisors to comment on these improvements, and the president was delighted to learn that most comments were complimentary.

After the tour, they all settled in the conference room to discuss the aims and objectives of the visitation. They had completed only half of the agenda when Hardwood's secretary came in to give him a note.

"Gentlemen, our lunch is being served," he stated. "I suggest we go eat it while it is hot."

"Harold, can't we postpone the lunch for a few moments? I feel we are beginning to get to the heart of things," said the president.

"We can do that, sir," said Harold, "but there is no way to keep the food warm, and the caterers will take it back in 15 minutes if we don't show up. They can sell it in the plant down the road."

Lunch consisted of thinly sliced warm roast beef, potatoes, and beans, accompanied by tasteless coffee. All of it was served on paper plates with plastic eating tools. The caterer had left earlier to make his appointment at Valiant Industries, two blocks away. There were no napkins.

A. C. Bustle ate with his customary cheerful banter, but the president said nothing.

When the meal was completed, the men returned to the conference room and finished the meeting. As the president was stepping into the Cadillac to return to the plane, he turned to Hardwood and smiled. "As I said, Harold, I think your operation is running very smoothly here. I am very pleased and encouraged. I feel that you and your staff have been most cooperative. All of you are major assets to Big Daddy, Inc.

"However, there are a couple of things that I don't quite understand—that horrible lunch for one thing, and this fine automobile with bed sheets in it. Somehow they don't seem to go along with the impression of efficiency I received from the rest of your operation. Also, I would like to get more information about that new warehouse you rented on the other side of town."

A. C. Bustle cleared his throat. "Perhaps," he said, "Harold wouldn't mind if I explained those items on the way to the airport."

"Not at all, A. C.," smiled Harold, "be my guest. And we will look forward to seeing you again in the very near future."

And they lived happily ever after.

Comment:

The Outgo management will continue to run their company with a minimum of interference. The ground rules have been set. A. C. Bustle and his staff know that they can be more effective in other areas. I doubt that they will want to tangle with Outgo again. Survival was threatened by the merger. Counterthreat was poised. And the two canceled each other.

A couple of corollaries are present:

1. The most consistent survivors always tell the truth and deal sincerely, as far as anyone can tell.

2. A man with only one cow will never let it go.

LAW NO. 2
A person's loyalty is a function of how much he feels he is appreciated.

It seems like every time I pick up a business magazine, there is an article or comment on the problem of the "transient executive." Prominent managers are quoted as saying that the problem of keeping good men is the primary one facing business today. Then a discussion of profit sharing, stock options, and other compensation plans is held. The purpose of the article is to show that top management is really into the situation and is taking the necessary steps to correct it. The solution, it seems, is merely a matter of providing the right amount of money to ensure executive loyalty and hard work.

Apparently these men have never taken a look at themselves, or if they have, they feel that the rest of the world is different. People don't work for money. They work for appreciation. Now obviously I don't mean that executives aren't interested in money. Certainly they are. But their interest in it has little to do with the amount of work they accomplish, or the loyalty they possess. Once a man is making a living wage and has some practical vision of security in his mind, he really casts financial things aside in terms of his job. The real money difference between the $20,000 you are making and the $25,-000 a competitor is offering is almost invisible. By the time you move, it is all gone. Even if you don't move, it is all gone.

Stock plans are set up for retirement or death. No reasonable person believes that either one of these will actually happen to him; so he is concerned only with the present. For the present, we like to be appreciated. Strangely enough one of the least effective methods of showing appreciation is money. Of all the things money is, the main thing it isn't is personal. The numbers on a check represent no personal commitment or interest from the senior executives of the organization. They're just numbers. Money isn't money until you spend it. Just like a bell is no bell till you ring it (with apologies to Oscar Hammerstein). So if the item of recognition is not something you can touch, or feel, then it doesn't exist, except as a scoring device.

We all know of children given everything by their parents except personal attention and understanding. Contemporary fiction is filled with stories of neglected families, heartbroken wives, and lonely grandmothers. Love itself is recognition and appreciation. Lack of appreciation can destroy it. (Hell hath no fury, etc.) Executives get lonely, too, and when they get lonely, they start thinking about themselves and how mistreated they are. That is when they start polishing up the old résumé to embark on an industry-wide search for appreciation

Box 3477
Wall Street Journal
New York, New York

Dear Sirs,

I am responding to your advertisement in yesterday's paper concerning your need for an Engineering Program Manager. My detailed résumé is attached. I have been with my present employer for 5 years. As you know, he is in the same type of business you are.

Naturally you will be interested in why I plan to change jobs. I could provide you with several traditional reasons, but in order to assure that we understand each other, I should explain something to you.

In the 5 years I have been here, I have had a raise every year and my bonus has risen proportionately. Travel expenses are generous, and my relationships with my boss are good, although we don't see each other with much frequency.

But it is very difficult here to communicate upward. There is no way to find out how you are doing except by asking, and there is no way to offer a new idea without making an issue of it.

Last month my boss asked me to cancel a long-planned audit trip to make a special visit to a major supplier who was having a lot of trouble. It was difficult on such short notice to cancel out and required a major diplomatic effort on my part. But it was done. I spent a week at the supplier's plant, and we got most of the problems ironed out. I went back with a feeling of accomplishment.

However, in trying to report on the emergency trip, I had great difficulty getting in to see my boss. He was tied up. When I finally got into his office the next day and started to show him the results of the visit, he looked at me blankly.

"Oh yes," he said, "I forgot to tell you. We decided last Thursday to just cancel these people out. They've been too much trouble over the years. I meant to tell you, but it slipped my mind. However, the trip was good experience for you."

Now it is obvious to me that this is a company that doesn't feel it needs me very badly. If I hadn't gone to see him, I could have been working on that problem forever without knowing that it was all over.

So before we start discussing my coming to work with your company, I would like to make sure that you have better communication practices than these I have just described.

Very truly yours,

So far we have listed some of the things that appreciation isn't. What are some of the things that it is? The most important thing that appreciation is is the opportunity for personal contribution and the recognition that goes with the acceptance or rejection of this contribution. Some might raise their eyebrows at the suggestion that appreciation could be associated with rejection of a person's ideas or deeds. Yet we have all seen men struggle harder (that might be a good advertising slogan) to overcome rejection than they have struggled to achieve recognition in the first place.

If all else fails, you can resort to the use of professionalism. But first you must understand, "Why is professionalism?"

Why do specialists go to such lengths to require certification, examination, and oath-taking from those who would enter their profession? Why do engineers differentiate between "degree men" and "practice men"? Why do universities establish so many levels of titles, and why does the military hang insignia on their people? To inform or protect the public? To improve communications? It ain't necessarily so.

All these devices exist for the same and sole basic reason: instant respect. The only titles used regularly are those which convey the bearer's status and knowledge immediately. You run into many "doctors," "colonels," "professors," etc., in your daily life. How often do you meet someone billing himself as "private first class," "merchant," or "room clerk"?

"Gloria, I would like to present Dr. S. Lyndon Walker." Ah, romance and interest are in the air before a word has been spoken. "Vice-president" used to be a pretty good status title in most companies, but now we have senior vice-presidents, executive vice-presidents, and even senior executive vice-presidents. When introduced to a mere vice-president now, people usually ask, "Vice-president of what?"

Therefore, if you are to show your appreciation to those executives you would like to keep, you must take this phenomena into consideration. A title is worth several raises provided you make sure that other people understand the dignity contained therein. The truly inventive boss can keep everyone happy and recognized without much trouble if he learns how to handle the title tree. I suggest omitting regent, führer, and similar designations. They sometimes get out of hand.

LAW NO. 3
The amount of accurate information an executive possesses concerning the status of his operation varies inversely with his position in the organization.

The bigger your job and the more influence you possess over the lives and future of your associates, the less unfiltered information you will receive. This occurs due to two beliefs held by every subordinate:

1. "It is not to my advantage to voluntarily tell my superiors things that place my judgment, competence, or actions in an unfavorable light."

2. "The boss has more information than I do. He must know what is happening. If he doesn't care, then why should I worry?"

The love of accurate data has produced a whole new industry: management systems. The glamor companies of today are those utilized to support and create management information. Computers, copiers, and communications equipment all exist because managers feel that they must have instant information. Companies spend millions of dollars establishing systems to automatically introduce all cost and service items into a central computer system. The information is programmed, analyzed, and transmitted to all interested managers. Copies are made, and every executive has the vital data before him faster than a speeding bullet.

Although it is both fast and bountiful, it usually consists of the same old filtered stuff. Output data can be no more refreshingly accurate than the input data from which it is concocted. Input data is always filtered. (Law No. 1 explained that.) To help us understand why it is filtered, we should examine one portion of the completed data package lying before the company president. Suppose we take a noncomplex item —one that couldn't involve any filtered information, something straightforward and measurable, like finished goods inventory. All you have to do to determine finished goods inventory is count the finished items not yet sold or delivered. In fact, our mythical information system has set up a method whereby a card is filled out each time an item enters or leaves the finished goods inventory. This card is put into the computer. The arithmetic is accomplished, and we know precisely what this inventory is. Right? Not necessarily. Although the print out lying on the desk says that we have 34,182 items in finished goods inventory, we really have 83,139. Seems some product line managers have learned about "accruals." Accrual is a method whereby you take credit for goods ordered but not yet delivered or paid for. It is a poor relation of the float system used by banks. When you deposit an out-of-town check, your bank won't let you draw any money on it for 3 or 4 days while they have it verified and accomplish their bookkeeping. However, during these 3 or 4 days, they are busily lending out that very money, or money that it backs. They don't admit this. When the new interbank communication systems eliminate the float, economic terror will stalk the business houses.

A production manager, faced with criticism for producing too much, knows that to produce less he must get rid of people. He also knows that having once eliminated these workers, he will be faced with a higher overhead and the difficult problem of replacing said workers when the time comes to increase output. Therefore, he cops out. He allocates certain production to the turnover inherent in a large distribution system. It's there, but you can't find it. Conversely, when the inventory threatens to get a little low, he reduces the amount charged to accrual, and by magic it grows.

The top executives, poring over the numbers supplied by their system, are left with a feeling of contentment. The staff people, who know what is really going on, are unable to communicate this to topside because they would have to explain why the system doesn't know this. It is all very disconcerting.

There is a corollary to Law No. 3 that applies to parents as well as business executives: If you don't ask the right question, you don't get the right answer.

It is only fair to ask what filtered information means. My Gawd, what if the United States government, and particularly the Department of Defense, had to rely on such things? Can you imagine what would happen to us? (Ever hear of Bull Run, Pearl Harbor, the Bay of Pigs, etc.?)

No one is really bad. It is just that we all have different ideas concerning what "good" is. Each person feels that those to whom he is reporting information require some assistance in interpreting it, so he places that interpretation in the report and allows it to appear as fact. Consider some examples:

"We are going to need 20 additional people to finish the work by Thursday." (Translation: I only need six but you are going to cut me to that anyway.)

"Our competition is telling everyone that they are going to cut prices 25 percent next month." (Translation: I had a lousy trip.)

"Engineering is working on a new design that will eliminate this problem" (Translation: We haven't been able to solve it here; so we are passing it along.)

"Tell it like it is" has become a slogan for the youth of today. "Tell it like it ought to be" is the slogan of reporting managers. Let he who is without translation cast the first termination slip.

LAW NO. 4
The effectiveness of any program depends upon the amount of participation delegated.

No one can do the job as well as I.

Let us admire, applaud, and accept that statement. Now let us regretfully discard it. Anyone can do the job all by himself, but the ones who make the big money are those who can get others to do the job for them, while enjoying every minute of it. (A la Tom Sawyer.)

We can all recognize from our personal experience that very few managers are able to accomplish this task. Things do get done and done well, if enough attention and pressure are applied. But the only way they get done inexpensively, continuously, and effectively is if every person involved feels that he is a primary contributor and that it is necessary for him to lead the way by example and accomplishment.

In short, the successful manager knows how to accomplish participation without making a big deal of it. Let's consider two separate organizations: Each is interested in establishing a program to assure that the purchases made in multiple locations are accomplished according to standard practices, maximum efficiency, and general all-around "wonderfulness."

The first organization creates a new senior purchasing group. The group then writes a purchasing manual, conducts training courses among the purchasing people throughout the organization, and establishes auditors to continually survey the operations to be sure that they are following the manual to the letter. The reports of the auditors are circulated, and each responsible location is required to explain its incidents of lack of compliance. A training coordinator is hired. Courses are developed in those procedures noted to be least utilized, and affected personnel are trained. The result is improved measurement, better coordination, and more unified purchasing operations. However, the expense of the managing group, training program, and audit eats up the savings produced.

The second organization creates a senior purchasing executive only—no group. He brings together those managers responsible for purchasing at the separate locations and presents them with the problem.

"Gentlemen," he says, "I have been asked to find a way to improve our effectiveness. Obviously I do not know how to do this. However, I think that together we can accomplish it. I would like your suggestions and guidance on how to proceed."

Within a few moments, it becomes apparent that the steps necessary are to (1) identify the problem now faced, (2) determine their causes, and (3) conduct the proper system controls and training to eliminate the problems.

The operating managers distribute the assignments among themselves. The investigation proceeds. Within a few months, there is a large improvement at virtually no cost, and the improvement continues.

Why is the second method more effective than the first? Only one reason—it creates an environment of participation. This environment can only be developed through good intentions, patience, and delegation of responsibility. Strong guidance, little direction, and a transference of importance are the techniques of participation. Specific direction, lecture discussions, and controlled training are the techniques of non-participation.

The rewards of a participation program are obvious to a Situation Manager: (1) The overhead is low; (2) ideas and the bodies to achieve them are willingly given; and (3) when any-thing goes wrong, a lot of people share the blame.

People really do not respond when presented with a com-pleted program guaranteed to produce "instant success." They recognize instinctively that if success is achieved, recognition will go to the program, while if nothing significant happens, it will be considered their fault for not implementing those words of wisdom properly. Therefore, they fight it.

It is considered knowledgeable in management to speak of the NIH (not invented here) factor. Everyone recognizes that it is difficult to transmit perfectly acceptable ideas to another organization because of this phenomenon. What they do not recognize is that such a response is inevitable. It is not just a story or a joke. It is inevitable.

Therefore, the wise Situation Manager will arrange to sup-ply no more than a framework and insist that the personnel involved fill in the blanks. A properly arranged framework can produce the same results as the original program. The dif-ference is that there will now be participation, a sense of au-thorship, and dedication on the part of those involved.

It's not "What's in it for me?" that concerns people, it's "How much of me is in it?"

LAW NO. 5
The less systematic support a decision maker receives, the better decisions he will make.

The industrial might of the world was built (rightly or wrongly) by individual men. They all possessed the virtues of strong will, absolute dedication, and determination to achieve some goal. They possessed some nonvirtues, too, but that is not our problem.

These men personally controlled every part of their opera-tion. If a decision had to be made on finance, marketing, quality, manufacturing, horticulture, or anything else—they made it. The measure of their success in making these decisions on a minute by minute basis is whether or not their company was successful.

Today this system of management is unacceptable because everyone owns the companies and most managers are professionals instead of entrepreneurs. These professionals have developed management systems to provide volumes of data in order to help them make decisions. (Note Law No. 3.) As a result, so many facts are available that the decision is virtually made before the executive ever receives the opportunity to go through his pondering act.

The net result is: All decisions are made based on what occurred in the past.

Now I yield to no one in my respect for the knowledge and experience gained in the past. In fact, one of my hobbies is trying to place stories from the front page of the Sunday *New York Times* at another point in history. Very little new happens in man's political history. Only the names change.

But business events are not political events. Forms of government may occur, disappear, and reoccur, but forms of transportation are not likely to do so, nor is electronic technology. Henry Ford, Thomas Edison, Alexander Bell, and their like could not have passed a modern management system analysis. No precedents.

"But," you say, "I am not trying to create a new industry. I just want to determine the best place to put a new plant. Surely the information accumulated by the local utilities and other agencies will help me make this decision?" Help? Yes. They will help you based upon the skill of their technical writers and their public relations firm. After all, how many places are bad? There are successful operations everywhere, and right next door to them are unsuccessful activities.

What really matters is where you want it. Then it will work.

It is acceptable luncheon conversation to speak of the ineffectiveness of committees. It is well known, for instance, that the only color a committee can agree on is beige.

Yet the instinct for assembling committees is so strong that few can resist.

What produces this instinct? The feeling that a group might make a better, or at least safer, decision than an individual? They only make better decisions when said decision has already been arranged and planted by one person.

Imagine the captain of a ship taking this step. Action is his responsibility and his alone. He knows it. Therefore, he makes command decisions automatically. Any normal individual placed in this position will be doing the same thing 10 minutes after coming aboard.

People rise to the challenge, if it is given. Their nature, however, is to drop to the standards of the group because it is safer there. The more information available, the broader the chain of command, the larger the opportunity to pass the responsibility along. I have no facts on it, but I would bet that you can assess the achievements of any general or admiral by finding out which ones had sent the least amount of messages requesting instructions from headquarters. Those who asked for the least help achieved more.

To accompany this analysis, it should be pointed out that the game is only successful when the consequences are serious. Those who make wrong decisions should be permitted to lose for real. Nothing sharpens the mind like that.

LAW NO. 6
Pride goes before all.

Why will a soldier charge up a hill in the face of overwhelming enemy fire? Because he knows he'll get into trouble if he doesn't? For mom's apple pie? For the girl next door?

Hardly. He goes up that hill, hating every step of the way,

so that he won't look bad in front of his comrades. That's pride.

What makes a production foreman come to the plant in the middle of the night to make sure a behind-schedule job is getting done?

Why does a salesman bust his tail to go over his quota and win the contest? (It isn't the TV set he'll win.)

Why does a secretary make sure her boss's letters have no spelling or grammatical errors in them before they go out, even though it would be his fault?

Why will 800 intelligent people, who obviously have better things to do, sit in an uncomfortable elementary school gym to watch 400 kids sing Christmas Carols?

Why do people wear jewelry? Why do they discard their perfectly usable wardrobes to buy the latest fashion? Why were contact lenses invented?

Why do we want to fly first class even though it is more expensive?

Orientals, practical souls that they are, have long acknowledged the importance of "face," which is pride. They speak of it frankly and put a lot of thought into not causing others to lose it. This prevents many embarrassing situations.

Westerners somehow feel that being concerned with pride is unmanly. They relate to "pride in work," "pride in country," and so forth, but "pride in self" is considered some sort of emotional sin. They have learned that personal concern is considered vanity.

By not recognizing it openly, they are, therefore, forced to many devious schemes to show that they are not motivated by pride in self. Boys aren't supposed to show their pride has been hurt. Girls must remain poised at all times.

All of us are expected to endure stoically any of the personal put downs that come our way. It is okay to react to physical insult but not to soul insult.

When personal pride is involved, people will walk firmly

down a path they know is wrong, and that they know other people know they know is wrong, before they would give in and let anyone know their feelings were hurt.

Since you cannot speak of your pride, or state frankly that your pride has been dented, there is very little chance that anyone will notice your problem. As such it sits there and boils, only to erupt when a totally unrelated situation arises and provides an opportunity for revenge.

This is, in my opinion, the prime reason for the high failure of marriages and other close relationships. Since such a delayed reaction makes it impossible to always understand another's apparent overreaction to the current incident, communications stop.

To overcome the pride factor in Situation Management, you must force a communication with the other person—but on an indirect basis.

You don't hand someone a bottle of mouthwash; you tell him about the wonderful one you discovered.

You don't tell someone he is wrong. You give him a book on the subject, since he is well known as having an open mind.

Above all, you don't get involved with or disturb another person's prerogatives or mess around in his territory without his invitation.

Embarrassed kittens become tigers.

Fear of being left out, fear of rejection, fear that inadequacies will become known—these are the motivators of the pride that leads us astray. Because of these, the proud person may choose not to participate rather than face the consequences.

Before beginning to resolve a situation caused by another's pride, all good Situation Managers make sure that their own pride is not the one at fault.

LAW NO. 7
A job can only be successful as the
means supplied to measure it.

All bets are made on the first tee.

The successful Situation Manager is one who learns to establish the ground rules for success before launching himself into completing the job assigned to him. If nothing else, he must assure himself that he will know when he is finished. He must also decide what persons are involved in deciding he is finished, and supply them with the means to measure his progress.

Much of the tragedy of modern life is wrapped up in the failure to accomplish those two basic steps. Yet it is a normal pattern in our nonbusiness life. A golf course has 18 holes. A football field has goal lines. Parties have a time established for beginning and ending. Airplanes go from city to city. The list goes on.

Yet an amateur Situation Manager will accept an assignment to "go straighten out the problem in Cleveland" without establishing simple agreements, such as "What problem?" or "Which Cleveland?" Consequently, he works his little heart out and returns to be considered inadequate.

You are going to be measured anyway by some means, fair or foul. Usually the one doing the measuring has nothing specific in mind; so he does it by the seat of his pants. Careers are destroyed in this manner. It is the situation equivalent to "Let's have lunch sometime."

When there are no measurements called out at the start of the action, any of the players can keep score or call the game at his discretion. Therefore, it is incumbent upon the junior person to establish the rules.

The situation in Cleveland will be fixed when what events

occur? What minds are changed to believe what? What product or service is accomplished that did not exist before?

If this rule could be established in world diplomacy, there would be far fewer conflicts. Consider the way it is handled now when the republic of AABAR gets upset with the republic of ZZAND. "You are not observing the treaty," says the minister of AABAR. "We are too," replies the minister of ZZAND. "You are not." Sabers are taken from the footlockers. Lights burn late at night, and the cabinets meet to consider the problem. AABAR notes that ZZAND has mobilized its guard regiments. Consequently, they put some gasoline in their airplane. This brings a further escalation by ZZAND in that they declare a state of emergency and lock up all who are opposed to the government. Each entreats the United Nations to help against the opposing forces of tyranny.

If some cool head in the UN asks what the problem is, he will be told the details of military preparation conducted by the other. The treaty, whatever it was, has been forgotten.

Any legitimate assignment must contain a definable purpose and a practical measurement of progress. To accept one otherwise is to do a disservice to yourself and to the person handing it out.

Of course, you want to be the one keeping track of the status.

ASSIGNMENT: Get a better turnout at the next PTA meeting.

The key item is knowing how many people were at the previous meetings. That way you know the amount of members you need to attract in order to accomplish your mission. Make a simple flow chart showing what the attendance has been in the past, and mark your accomplishment on it. It will be obvious to the world that you have been successful.

ASSIGNMENT: Eliminate the problem of long lines at the cafeteria.

The key item is, of course, to obtain a documented count of how long the lines are now. An even more accurate measurement would be to determine the average waiting time. Then get agreement on a desirable waiting time. When you meet or beat that time, you are done.

ASSIGNMENT: Get a better grade in English.

ASSIGNMENT: Find out why Apex Machine Company doesn't buy from us anymore.

ASSIGNMENT: A secret organization is trying to take over the government of Zambelia. Stop them. If any members of your team are killed or captured, the secretary will deny any knowledge of your activities.

LAW NO. 8
People are more important to situations than things.

In 1812, Napoleon marched his troops into Moscow. Except for minimum damage caused by fires set by the retreating Russians, the city was almost intact. There were, however, no people in the Russian capital except Napoleon and his group. Some days later he marched out again, hoping to beat the Russian winter and starvation, back across the frontier. He had learned that a city is people, not things.

The same is true in the art of Situation Management. Things will rarely cause problems for you of their own volition. They do not have the ability to scheme, plot, or act. People, however, do. Things come and go (it has been stated that 90 percent of the things we use in our daily life did not exist in 1900), but people stay much the same.

Plutarch told about the conditions in Athens 500 years before Christ: "The disparity of fortune between rich and poor had reached its height, so that the city seemed to be in a truly dangerous condition, and no other means for freeing it from disturbances . . . seemed possible but despotic power. The poor, finding their situation worse with each year—the government and the army in the hands of their masters, and the corrupt courts deciding every issue against them, began to talk of violent revolt, and a thoroughgoing redistribution of wealth. The rich, unable any longer to collect debts legally due them, and angry at the challenge to their savings and their property, invoked ancient laws, and prepared to defend themselves by force against a mob that seemed to threaten not only property but all established order, all religion, and all civilization." (Sounds like the *New York Post*.)

That description could apply to conditions in almost every country at some time during its development. Portions of it apply to the thinking of some groups today. Its ablution has been approached by violence, by invasion, by coalitions, and by ignoring the whole thing. The best solution was found by the man brought in to solve the problem of Athens—Solon. He canceled all the debts, freed people sold into slavery for debt, and barred such arrangements in the future. Suddenly the Athenians found themselves with nothing to fight about. Solon had placed his finger squarely on the seat of emotion and with one masterful stroke wiped out the pet hate of everyone at the same time. The system was unfair. He removed it.

Those who attempt to resolve similar situations by concentrating on things alone would have set about redividing the land and redistributing the wealth until each person had approximately the same amount of things. Of course, within a few years, the distribution would become as before, since the smart or greedy always triumph in that aspect. Instead of things, he gave them dignity and a new start.

In our personal situations, we are always faced with the decision of concentrating our efforts on things (the computer is giving wrong answers) or people (the computer is being programmed incorrectly). Things are easier to manage than people, in the mind of the novice Situation Manager. Unfortunately, although things seem to cause problems, they do not express financial or brotherly gratitude once the situation is past. What is the use of solving a situation if nobody knows of your brilliance?

The mature Situation Manager goes where the action is. Action is something that pleases you, like money, appreciation, promotion, or recognition. Unless you get your big kicks from an electric massage, there is nothing things can do for you that people can't improve on.

LAW NO. 9
Improvement is the only practical management goal.

At annual report time around the management world, the call goes out for suggestions concerning goals to be accomplished by the organization during the forthcoming year. Said goals must be specific so that they can be measured.

I wonder what the stockholders would say if some of the following goals were submitted:

REDUCE PROFIT BY 13.67 PERCENT DURING THE COMING YEAR

INCREASE SALARIES OF ALL OFFICERS BY 45 PERCENT

SHORTEN WORK DAY BUT MAINTAIN CURRENT WAGES

ADD 18 ADDITIONAL HOLIDAYS

It is possible that all these goals could be explained in a manner that would show them to be for the good of the company. If so, it would probably be accomplished by a new management team.

It is only practical to be concerned with improvement. To propose regression is fatal. All of this, of course, is a matter of our environment. We live in an age of bigger and better achievements. Little that has been accomplished before is relative.

We are tilted into the trap of needing to improve when potty training starts, and never end it until we are presented (not to our knowledge) with a bigger and better funeral than any other member of the family until then.

Improvement is a disease, but it is vital for survival as Situation Managers.

There is, however, one bright spot. Not everyone is able to recognize improvement when he sees it. It follows then that one cannot necessarily recognize a slideback when it occurs. People who arrange improvement are called economists. Preferably they are employed by the party in power at the moment.

LOSSES WERE REDUCED BY $645,729 DURING THIS REPORTING PERIOD.

(Of course we still dropped 7 million dollars.)

Therefore, if we are to achieve survival and triumph as Situation Managers, we must learn to look at everything in terms of improvement, regardless of its total effect. Assuredly, the automobile was an improvement over the horse. Yet if you are required to make a case for explaining why the company's vehicles were repossessed, you can come out for smog abatement and declare that you are returning to the horse-drawn van as one step in this direction.

Should the accountant abscond to Brazil with the funds and a secretary, you can point out that the overhead has been reduced by two people.

But it is wise to recognize that no one wants to acknowledge the realities of lack of progress. There are times when such a lack may be the best step, but it must be disguised.

Gaining weight adds dignity to a man, like gray hair. Surely that is improvement.

LAW NO. 10
Nobody really listens.

"Stay out of that tree. You'll break an arm."
"Walk."

"Don't walk."

"If you carry your money in cash, you'll lose it."

"Put on a sweater, or you'll catch your death of cold."

"A penny saved is a penny earned."

"A fool and his money are soon parted."

"If you marry that girl, you'll regret it for the rest of your life."

"To get a good job, get a good education."

"Don't try to pet a strange dog. He will bite you."

"Do unto others as you would have others do unto you."

"Look before you leap."

"Neither a borrower nor a lender be."

"Marry in haste, repent at leisure."

"A torn jacket is soon mended, but hard words bruise the heart of a child."

"An infallible way to make your child miserable is to satisfy all of his demands."

"Never put off until tomorrow that which you can do today."

"None have more pride than those who dream that they have none."

"We flatter ourselves that we desert our vices when in reality they desert us."

"Few save the poor feel for the poor."

"What a man won't do for his girlfriend, he sure won't do for his wife."

"Never take yourself off the payroll."

and so on.

Santayana wrote, "Those who cannot remember the past, are condemned to repeat it."

How strange it seems that with all the advice provided to succeeding generations throughout the history of man that people keep making the same mistakes. The only difference is the broader opportunity for error offered by the advances of technology.

A child burns his fingers on the stove and looks tearfully up to his mother just as the caveman's son did. After fixing the hurt, the mother is bound to remind him that she carefully explained how touching one's hand to the hot area would cause it to be burned. "You didn't listen."

How many people do you suppose drown every year because they swam energetically immediately after eating? Surely everyone knows that the food needs to digest.

Speed is still a main cause of automobile accidents. In junk lots, refrigerator doors are still trapping little children. Bad accounting practices are still causing business failures.

There are volumes full of the wisdom of the past, and most of it is carefully read by each following generation. Yet individuals still have to learn everything by themselves. Surely this is the cause of the perennial "generation gap."

There are two reasons why people don't listen: They don't think that the item under discussion affects them or they think that their judgment is superior to that of the talker.

As a result, we careen through life bouncing off that experience, hurdling this one, scratching our way over another, and continuing until we have gained enough wisdom to croak it into the ear of an unbeliever.

Situation Management is not about to change the nature of man. If people want to start over again with each birth, that is their business. Our business is to recognize that if we want them to understand something, we must work very hard to explain it, and we must be sure that we are reaching them.

You cannot take your message of wisdom and just hurl it out to the world knowing that it will be appreciated for itself and taken immediately to heart. You must arrange that your message has a personal impact on the life style of the listener.

Obviously it is impractical to withhold food or comfort from him until he can recite your words in perfect sequence. That not only doesn't assure understanding but may get you into trouble. You can withhold love or honor, but that technique is restricted by how many people care whether you love or honor them.

Recognize it. You must concentrate very hard to get a true listener. I hope that if you find one, you will be kind enough to share him with me.

The Situation of the Boss versus Peace and Quiet

The big boss has just accused you of having an out-of-control situation in your department. You know this is not true. What do you do now? (This situation is to prepare you for the Situation Analysis format.)

You (Harry Jennings) are the quality control manager in a large company. For you everything is coming up roses. There are no major nonconformance problems. Production is moving out the door on schedule. The customers are happy with the product, and the engineering department has just agreed to install a new drawing control system that will make your job even easier. All is well with your world. You have been firm but fair, and the company is far ahead of where it was when you came. Costs are down. Product quality is up. You are a happy man, Harry Jennings.

As you stroll to the executive dining room you turn a corner and there before you, with fire in his eyes, is the "big boss." He sees you; he steps forward; he speaks: "Jennings, all I have been hearing about are the quality problems on the stuff we get from our suppliers. It seems to me that we shouldn't have these problems if your department is doing its job. I'd like to hear how you intend to fix this situation. Put it on the schedule for the staff meeting tomorrow."

Without waiting for an answer he stomps off.

What are you going to do now, Harry? Your bonus, your reputation, and possibly your job are in danger. (Law No. 1 rears.) You don't know of any big suppliers' problems. Or have *they* been lying to you? Should you:

1. Rush back to the office, call your guys responsible for suppliers' quality, and read them the riot act? They let you down.

2. Dust off your air travel card and head for the major suppliers' plants to see what they have been up to? (This way you might be able to avoid the staff meeting.)

3. Gather all the suppliers' data you can find, pore over it with your staff, and then create a chart-filled presentation for the meeting to show that things are in better shape than they have ever been?

4. Resolve to go to the meeting without any preparation and sit calmly, accepting any blame that might come along and asking for suggestions for improvement? (You know this will take the wind out of their sails.)

The question is which, if any, of these courses should be followed. Perhaps you might choose variations of the several. Heaven knows there are an infinite number of ways for a manager to place himself in a box.

The veteran Situation Manager knows, however, that he must think before he acts. This is particularly true when people who have a direct influence on your career, reputation, prestige, or peace of mind are involved. Since that involves almost everyone, it becomes plain that things must be thought out.

So you retire to a quiet spot and start to ask yourself some questions.

Q.   Why am I so concerned?

A.   The big boss is upset with me.

Q.   Why is he upset?

A.   Because the suppliers are out of control.

Q.   Is that what he said?

A.   No. He said, "All I have been *hearing* about are the quality problems on the stuff we get from our suppliers."

Q.   You make out the official problem reports. You don't remember any big suppliers' problems; and besides, you haven't talked with him for a month. So where did he hear it?

A.   Let's find out who he has been talking to.

Having reached this point, you review your thinking to make sure it is sound. Then, just in case, you call your supplier quality men and you ask them how things are going. "Never better," they reply. Further questioning produces no indication of trouble or loss of faith. There must be another source, and their information must be questionable, or perhaps yours is wrong.

First stop—purchasing department.

Cal Foster, the purchasing manager, is sitting quietly at his desk trying to work his way through the "in" basket. He smiles as you come in but does not appear overwhelmed with emotion at your visit. After bringing each other up-to-date on family health, vacation plans, and local gossip, you casually approach the subject of suppliers' problems.

To your surprise Foster immediately plunges into a list of the virtues of your people who have been working with his buyers. Seems that things have never been running so smoothly, although he thinks *you* could speed things by a quicker receiving inspection.

His chief buyer sticks his head in the office at that moment and with little invitation immediately recites the same speech, including the part about speeding up receiving inspection. You resist the temptation to suggest that they order sooner, thank them in a gentlemanly manner, and proceed. They don't seem to have any problems that would warrant such an uprising by the old man. Perhaps we'd better give this another "think."

Q. Who would be affected by defective products from suppliers?

A.a. Purchasing—because it would cause them to miss their schedules in delivering to manufacturing.

b. Manufacturing—because it would delay their work or cause them some rework costs.

c. Sales—because late deliveries would provide them with a loss of face to the customers, and they always are overoptimistic anyway.

d. Customers—if the defect were found too late, because they'd find it and blame us.

e. Finance—because the rework, warranty, and scrap costs would go up.

Q. Do you intend to spend your whole life on this situation? You've only got 24 hours before the meeting. What's a better approach?

A. I could find out where the big boss got his information.

Q. Great! All you have to do is ask him. How are you going to do that?

A. Without asking him.

Armed with this reasoning, you march down the hall to the secretary of your antagonist and explain that he has asked you to check some facts for him (true), but you are not sure of the source (true) and don't want to bother him (true). So, could she fill you in on his schedule for the past 2 or 3 days, and maybe then you could figure out who he has been spending his time with?

She knows you're in trouble, and you know she knows. However, she informs you that if you hadn't missed the previous staff meeting, you would have known that the big boss had spent the last 3 days at the annual sales meeting in Chicago and had just gotten back that morning.

"Whom did he travel with?" you ask; and she gives you the list. To nobody's surprise, it contains only salesmen.

Bob Blandford, the sales manager, is happy to see you. After stressing the fact that you exist only to serve him, you pop the important questions: "How do you feel our supplier quality program is going? Do you know of any significant problems in that area?"

Does he? "Do you realize," he demands to know, "that we lost 13 important sales on the wigit five line this quarter because our input feeder, made by Glick and Sons, doesn't have a reaction time fast enough for our customers? It's too slow by 30 percent. You guys have to get these people on the ball. If they can't make it right, then let's get someone else or make it ourselves."

He stands up and approaches the blackboard, chalk in hand, to give you the full lecture. Hastily you stop him to explain that the Glick and Sons' unit works just like the requirements given them and that you doubt if the rest of the equipment could accept the information that fast anyway.

Blandford indicates that engineering gave him the same story, but that he has to sell what the customers want, and that perhaps we'd all better get with the state of the industry.

At this point we'll impose a little suspended animation in order to provide thinking time. Obviously this is the source that the big boss found for his information. Just as obviously the problem does not lie with the supplier or your people. However, he is speaking the truth and something should be done. The question is: How do you get done what must be done and, at the same time, get yourself off the hook the boss has got you on without making a permanent enemy of the sales manager, Harry?

After a prolonged discussion, you prevail on Blanford to invite the engineering manager to the meeting. The three of you plan an item for the staff meeting; and, using your new-found influence with the boss's secretary, you manage to have it placed first on the agenda.

At the staff meeting Blanford makes a brief presentation which states that, although the present product meets the current specifications in all respects, it is necessary to consider a redesign to speed up the system. He urges that engineering be authorized to proceed and that, after the basic specification has been developed, the same suppliers be asked to participate in the system creation since they have been doing such a fine job on the current product.

"Including Glick and Sons?" asks the big boss.

The sales manager stares at him in disbelief. "Certainly," he replies, "they are our most consistent supplier. High quality all the way."

The meeting continues and the supplier-quality item is never mentioned.

Analysis

We have seen how our novice Situation Manager extracted himself from this problem. Even so, he did lose a little face and a few points by permitting the situation to occur at all. The sympathetic soul will now comment that this man had little control over what the sales manager said to the boss; yet Harry Jennings let himself in for this situation because he did not take steps to prevent it. It is apparent from his conversations with the purchasing and sales managers that he had not been taking time to find out what was on their minds. Thirteen sales missed over a three-month period did not happen in one day. The sales manager must have been concerned before he finally spilled all to the boss. Regular visits from Harry would have turned this up. The problem's solution became apparent as soon as they had discussed it. That could have happened just as easily 2 months before.

Concerning the subject of supplier quality you can bet that Harry is headed for further trouble. He has not been communicating with purchasing and has been leaning on his people's reports excessively.

The most important aspect in preventing difficult situations is to establish a continuing relationship which encourages people to tell you the troubles they think they have with you, prior to telling others. If, by constant contact, you establish the relationship—and accept their problems in a positive manner—life will become easier.

The easiest way to train your fellow managers in this method is to make heroes of them every chance you get. Harry let the sales manager be the hero in the case study, but his motives were geared to save his own neck. Not noble perhaps, but effective.

Situation Analysis Guide

AWARENESS:

1. What seems to be the situation?_____

_____

_____

2. How did I find out that the situation existed?_____

_____

_____

3. What is the potential effect of this matter?_____

_____

_____

4. How serious is it?_____

5. How much time do I have to extricate myself?_____

_____

_____

EVALUATION:

1. What evidence leads me to believe that the situation exists?

_____

_____

_____

_____

2. What is the specific source of this evidence?_____

_____

_____

 Do I know that the evidence is factual?_____

_____

_____

_____

4. Could I list the steps that created the situation?_____

_____

_____

_____

_____

5. Whose mind must I change to resolve the problem?_____

_____

_____

6. What does that mind think now?_____

_____

_____

7. How will I know when the situation is resolved?_____

_____

_____

ACTION:

1. Join the key individuals and the key issues._____

_____

_____

2. Why do they believe this?_____

_____

3. What would it require to separate them from this belief?

_____

_____

4. What is the best method to use in this separation?_____

_____

_____

5. How do I implement the method?_____

_____

_____

6. Once it is over, what steps do I take to assure that it will never happen again?_____

_____

_____

_____

The ABC's of
Situation Management

The types of situations that concern us involve only relationships with people. We will leave the resolution of physical danger or appliance-malfunction problems to the adventure stories. They are best solved by reflexes, prayer, resolve, or a good mechanic. People-relationship situations require only some thought, consideration, and a plan for resolution.

As we toured through a day in Henry Jennings life, it became apparent that he thought before he acted. That is the key point in the entire exercise. A situation worthy of our attention and concern is also worthy of a thoughtful evaluation. Therefore, we need a guide to make sure that all the facts are considered, since it is possible that we may become emotional enough to forget some important considerations.

The first step in Situation Management is to separate yourself from the situation environment and study the thing. It is not necessary to fly off to Mexico. An office, a parking lot, a park, or even a phone booth will do nicely. All you need is a place free from distraction for a few moments. The results will be even clearer if you can make yourself write the answers.

Separate your thinking into three areas and consider them one at a time: awareness, evaluation, and action.

AWARENESS
1. What seems to be the situation?
2. How did I find out that the situation existed?
3. What is the potential effect of this matter?
4. How serious is it? (If it is minor, determine whether it has possibilities of gaining importance and magnitude.)
5. How much time do I have to extricate myself?

EVALUATION
1. What evidence leads me to believe that the situation exists?
2. What is the specific source of this evidence?
3. Do I know that the evidence is factual? If I don't know, how can I find out?
4. Could I list the steps that created the situation? Are any missing or vague?
5. Whose mind must I change to resolve the problem?
6. What does that mind think now?
7. How will I know when the situation is resolved?

ACTION
1. Join the key individuals and the key issues. (Try to get it down to one sentence.)
2. Why do they believe this?
3. What would it require to separate them from this belief? (Without creating another situation?)
4. What is the best method to use in this separation?

5. How do I implement the method?
6. Once it is over, what steps do I take to assure that it will never happen again?

If you ask yourself these questions, and listen carefully to the answers, you will have a good chance of resolving the situation in a craftsmanlike manner. However, you must be sure that you have the *whole* story, not just part of it; and you must be honest with yourself. (Watch out for Law No. 6.)

If you don't ask the right questions, you don't get the right answers. Let's examine our questions closer to make sure we will use them properly.

AWARENESS
1. *What seems to be the situation?*
We are all familiar with the "situation comedy" shows on radio and TV. "I Love Lucy" was probably one of the most successful. They all essentially follow the same format. First, a set of circumstances is described (the boss is being brought home to dinner); complications arise (unexpected house guests —usually unrefined); then, the action takes place (keeping everyone apart by feeding one group in the kitchen and one in the dining room—this causes the host and hostess to eat two meals at once), next, the confrontation (when everyone discovers everyone else and someone is insulted—bedlam reigns); and finally, a solution is produced and all is calm again.

Real-life plays are not too different. However, the situation is not exposed to you by a clever playwright; you must describe and identify it yourself. You are probably the only person who knows enough about it to do so. Therefore, you might use one paragraph to answer this first question of awareness:

■ I'm supposed to be at my son's graduation and at a business meeting in Miami on the same date. My family will kill me if I miss graduation. My associates will ruin me if I don't make that meeting.

■ My headache is really bothering me, I don't remember anything after the El Chico Club last night, and where did I get that big dog that is tied to the bottom of the bed?

■ At three o'clock tomorrow all the workers will line up for their pay, but our accounts receivable didn't come through this week. We have no money.

■ Here I stand in the center of a strange town. I lost my wallet and don't even have a dime to make a collect call to the office.

■ Where did I put that library book?

■ Two hundred and fifty-seven guests will arrive for the club meeting in fifteen minutes. The hotel forgot to take the steaks out of the freezer, and so dinner will be late. The speaker got here early and is in the bar completely smashed.

2. *How did I find out that the situation existed?*

■ You know you have failed to pay the electric bill when they shut off the lights.

■ You know that you are on bad terms with your girl friend when she refuses to answer the telephone and returns your letter, marked "deceased."

■ You begin to realize that a problem exists when the water in the bottom of the boat is equal with the level of the water in the lake.

This type of situation is apparent to even the most indifferent observer. The more complex the situation, the more unapparent it may be. That is why it is important to ask yourself how you found out the situation existed.

Did someone tell you? Did you smell it out yourself? When did you begin to have an inkling?

Harry Jennings was lucky; he was told directly and firmly that he had a problem. He got the message quickly. Most times you just become aware that things aren't going right.

You're beginning to get looks from people, looks that are not common to your everyday experience. You begin to act like the people in the bad breath commercial.

Consider the ancient truth that the "husband is always the last to know." There is only one reason for that. Everyone assumes that he already knows and that he doesn't care. So they don't tell him. The same is true in managerial life. The one involved may be the last to know.

If the husband doesn't find out, when only three people are involved, it is not too amazing, when hundreds of people may be involved, that a manager may suddenly find the walls coming down about his ears.

Therefore, it is important to the final solution to be able to state that your awareness of the situation came from somewhere. Your answer might be: I felt it, asked around, and there it was; my secretary told me; the boss hinted at it until I figured it out; I learned it in a bar from a stranger; my wife told my barber, etc. It doesn't make any difference really—it just matters that you know how you learned it.

3. *What is the potential effect of this matter?*

To prepare for the next question you must consider what can happen if the thing is not resolved. Harry decided that he might get fired, lose face, or possibly be downgraded. It might be that he was overreacting, but he did have that feeling.

As Situation Managers we should look at it in terms of how long the thing will persist if we don't do something about it and how residual the reaction will be.

Flagpole climbers have very little use for deodorants—they don't need them. Salesmen could be in deep trouble if they forgot. Eccentric millionaires can get by without paying their bills—somewhere there is a sympathetic lawyer the creditors can reason with. Salaried employees, regardless of rank, must not overlook theirs—a poor credit reputation is frowned upon.

Each situation must be considered in the personal light of the person it affects. The surest test of potential effect is the amount of uncomfortableness that the situation generates for you. If you don't make it go away, you will become even more pained.

4. *How serious is it?*

Now this is the heart of the matter. You must decide how much of your attention you are going to give it. Harry acted as though his situation were life or death, he may have over-reacted, but he felt that way.

The ability to recognize the significance or insignificance of a situation is a main skill of a Situation Manager. It takes just as much time to resolve something that is unconsequential as it does to tackle a monster. You must now decide.

Incidentally, in this matter of time, many managers say that they can't spare the time to think out and resolve situations because they have other things to do. I'd like to point out that those other things are unrecognized situations that will continue until given the proper attention. For instance:

"I have 23 hours of scheduled meetings a week." Who scheduled them? Who attends when you are on a trip? More than likely the meetings are on different subjects but with the same people. The situation here is serious—management is out of control. Needs a little agenda organization.

"You can't get good people anymore. Have to stay on them all the time." Who selected and trained them? People work to the level they think you expect. If they feel that you think they aren't reliable like their fathers (who probably also weren't), they won't be.

"I'll just ride with it. Bosses change so quickly around here that it doesn't matter anyway." Maybe they're looking for the right man, like one who can recognize and solve situations.

"It's always been that way." Probably will be until some-one changes it.

"I just don't have time to think." Got time to put gas in the car?

So classify your situation *serious* or *minor,* and treat it accordingly. If it is minor, move on to the next question. If you consider it serious, give a thought to what it could develop into. ("I'll be real good if you buy me a BB gun.")

5. *How much time do I have to extricate myself?*

This question may not be as simple as it sounds. Harry had 24 hours. He knew that because the boss told him so. The rules had been set for him. However, your particular set of circumstances may be different. The finality point might be vague; it may not exist to your knowledge. The only guidance I can provide is:

a. You probably have more time than you think you have.

b. Nobody does anything until just before the deadline anyway.

Therefore, consider that it must be resolved immediately, and do so. Otherwise you will put it off and will probably be faced with solving it in parallel with another situation. (No one ever believes this, but I felt that it should be said anyway.)

At this point, awareness should be complete. You have decided that a genuine situation exists, that you are involved, and that it is serious or has a potential of being serious in terms of disturbing your orderly life, and you know how much time you have to get out of it. Now let's start breaking it down into manageable segments, as they say in the PERT books.

EVALUATION

1. *What evidence leads me to believe that the situation exists?*

This may seem redundant since we have already talked about how we discovered the situation. However, the awareness portion does not necessarily lead to the methodical listing of facts. We must make sure that we have evidence besides subjective or emotional deductions. Surely no one must feel more foolish than the suspicious husband who bursts into his wife's parlor only to find her drinking tea with his mother. He may have been outsmarted; however, it will be some time before anyone takes his suspicions seriously again.

The usual evidence of situation existence is that other people think it exists. The more they tell you about it, or discuss it, the more you are inclined to believe it. But to avoid the twentieth century equivalent of "cry wolf" it is wise to document the main criteria in a short listing.

2. *What is the specific source of this evidence?*

There comes a time when you must present the facts to the jury. In this case the jury is you, and you are inclined to be sympathetic with yourself. However, evaluation exists only to see if it is necessary to take action. Therefore, you must answer the question specifically and precisely.

The value, of course, is in identifying the source in order to evaluate the factual weight of the case by measuring your confidence in his integrity.

3. *Do I know that the evidence is factual? (If I don't, how can I find out?)*

Assuming that now you have decided that the source is an honest one, we must recognize that even honest people can be mistaken. (Law No. 3) That is why legal systems develop courts of appeal whether people want them or not.

If any doubt exists, it is necessary to create a test. Harry probed the organization until he got a reaction. Separate fact from fiction before mounting your charger.

4. *Could I list the steps that created the situation? Are any missing or vague?*

Harry put together a train of events. After his preliminary investigation, he determined that the boss had spent some time with the sales manager following a disquieting session with customers. He could reconstruct the conversation that generated the statement of the big problem being supplier hardware. He could recognize that he had become the patsy. He could also recognize that everyone involved genuinely believed that he really was at fault.

However, if you cannot do this, if you find yourself glossing over spots in the story, then you better regroup and start over. Stories can be made to come out the way you want them just by manipulating the evidence. But that is fooling yourself.

5. *Whose mind must I change to resolve the problem?*

We have already discussed the thought that situations only involve people and their opinions. *Who* has to get his mind changed? As a part of this, several minds may require alteration; however, if you can start a chain reaction, the job becomes easier.

6. *What does that mind think now?*

Careful. Don't credit that mind with having all the information you possess. What does he really think? That you robbed a bank? That you were indiscreet? That you have been ignoring your responsibilities to play the horses? That you don't care?

Don't flail away at symptoms. Get to the meat of the deal.

7. *How will I know when the situation is resolved?*

The days of marching off with the princess and half the kingdom as a sign of successful situation solution are over. Your reward may be having the key to the executive washroom returned to you, or it may be an absence of rancor or attention.

But you must establish a measurement that will let you know when you have reached the end of the trail. You must know when you are done. Preferably that end should have a number in it or a prescribed statement. Samples of these might be:

"John, there'll be a $1,000 bonus for you next month."

"Marry me Alice, and I'll be the happiest man in the world."

"Carl, I was wrong on this item."

"You're right, George, it is 37 inches."

"Next time you fellows should check with Albert before you start talking about these things."

"How do you feel we should handle this in the future?"

"If all our operations were in this good shape, we'd have no problems."

ACTION

Evaluation and its daydreaming are over. Now it is time to become a man of action. What are we going to do about it? First we must condense the data to an action format. Let's see what Harry did.

1. *Join the key individuals and the key issues.*
   "The boss thinks our supplier control is bad, and he got that impression from the sales manager."

2. *Why does he believe this?*
   "He believes this because he knows he's got a problem, and this is the first reasonable cause that has been suggested."

3. *What would it require to separate him from this belief? (Without creating another situation?)*
   "It must be remembered that he is working on a problem that doesn't really exist; therefore, it cannot be solved. He must be made to know the real problem, so that we can act upon it. He must learn of this problem from the man who gave him the initial one. If this happens, we can move out on the real problem and forget the false one."

4. *What is the best method to use in this separation?*

"I must convince the problem source that he has not de-
fined the situation correctly; get him to recant (while saving
face); and let him provide constructive guidance for the company."

5. *How do I implement the method?*

"I get the principals together and help them deduce what
I already have figured out. Then together we present the
plan."

6. *Once it is over, what steps do I take to assure that it
will never happen again?*

"I will conduct regular meetings with my counterparts. If
they have a problem, I will know of it first."

The Situation of
the Little League Conspiracy

*P*aul Phillips was accosted by his nine-year-old son with the directness usually seen in small boys. "Dad," he blurted, "you just have to take the job. You have to get involved."

"Involved in what?"

"You have to agree to become president of the Little League, otherwise we won't have any teams and there won't be any games this year. Then I won't have any way to play baseball, and I'm just beginning to learn to hit the ball."

Paul calmed the youngster down long enough to find out that his colleagues had heard their fathers talking about how no one would take the job as president and that they would try to talk Paul into it.

"Never happen, son. There is no way they are going to get me into that thing. Sam Williams hasn't been the same since last season. Two years of it and the mothers had him worn right to the ground."

He pulled the boy to him and crouched so they were eye to eye.

"Do you realize that being a Little League president can destroy a man? Do you really want your father to be out there raking grass, keeping score, building fences, explaining to mothers that their boys can't play every inning and all that stuff?"

The boy thought about it and then looked his father in the eye as he said, "Yes."

When the delegation of managers and board members arrived to call on Paul that night, he quickly brushed them off and then served drinks to show he wasn't all bad.

"We're really not asking so much, Paul," said the spokesman, "The league requires that we have a president. Most of the guys want to be managers or coaches. We have lots of strong committees. There wouldn't be anything for you to do except to go to an area council meeting once in a while."

"And hand the mayor the first ball to be thrown out," volunteered another member.

Paul stood up and walked back and forth for a few moments.

"Gentlemen, let me give it to you straight. I won't go into my business obligations and my travel schedule. You all have that problem. And I'm not going to tell you that I'm not interested in Little League baseball, because I am. I think it is good for the kids. No, I'm not going to talk about all of those things."

"You already did," mentioned Tom Simmins.

Paul ignored the comment.

"What I am going to talk about is what I have seen while watching your last three presidents, none of whom are here tonight. I can only assume that they haven't been released from the rest home yet."

"Now that's not fair, Paul," said Tom, "We all work hard on this thing."

"I agree you all work hard, but you work hard on the games. The problems I am talking about are handling the equipment, collecting the money, preparing the fields, getting the sponsors, issuing uniforms, and all the things that I have seen the presidents do single-handedly. I tell you if I were president, I wouldn't do a damn thing; and if something didn't happen that some committee was supposed to do, I wouldn't run around fixing it. There just wouldn't be any game."

They all stood up and in one voice said: "Sold."

"What do you mean sold?" gasped Paul.

The chairman stepped forward.

"We are willing to meet your conditions. The board has agreed in advance to name you president and accept whatever conditions you name. Thank you, Paul, the kids appreciate it and so do we. The first full meeting is scheduled for next Wednesday at 7:30 P.M. in the school gym. I'll see you there."

And they disappeared.

The bedroom door was locked when Paul went down the hall.

"Let me in. What's the matter with you?" he shouted.

"You don't get in here until you get yourself out of that deal you just got yourself into," his wife cried. "I won't be able to go to the shopping center or anywhere without every woman in the area coming up to tell me how you are not treating her boy fairly."

She finally relented, but the atmosphere was quite cool.

Paul worried about this commitment and how it would interfere with other projects he wanted to accomplish. Physical labor was not his thing, nor was being a one-man administration. Yet he had to admit that, although people and their kids only got involved for the fun of baseball itself, there were a number of talented and dedicated men involved. Perhaps they would do their jobs if they had the proper reminder and motivation. Or would they?

Before getting an ulcer, he decided to take out a copy of the Situation Analysis guide to determine if he could come up with an escape route.

SITUATION ANALYSIS GUIDE

AWARENESS

1. What seems to be the situation? I have accepted a job as president in an organization where the president traditionally does all of the administrative and side jobs himself, in addition to being the whipping boy for hundreds of emotional parents.

2. How did I find out that the situation existed? I have watched the men who held this job over the years rushing around, taking verbal abuse, and generally not enjoying themselves.

3. What is the potential effect of this matter? It could worry me and cause me to lose some effectiveness. If I suffer what the others have suffered, my wife will make life tough for me. If I cop out, my son will be disappointed in me.

4. How serious is it? The meeting is 2 days from now, and I don't have a plan. If I don't have a plan, I'm dead.

5. How much time to I have to extricate myself? Two days.

EVALUATION

1. What evidence leads me to believe that the situation exists? Personal observation of my predecessors and the general knowledge that people aren't exactly campaigning for the job. If it is so easy and uncomplicated, how come one of them doesn't take it?

2. What is the specific source of this evidence? The committee itself said that it had been trying for some time to find a guy and that if I didn't take it, they couldn't play.

3. Do I know that the evidence is factual? I have witnessed all these things. In fact I even chewed poor Sam Williams out last year because I thought my son's manager was discriminating against him. I hope I am forgiven someday.

4. Could I list the steps that created the situation? Over the years, the administrative jobs have been casually treated compared to the game itself. Thus the men who were presidents assumed the tasks in order to assure that they were completed. After a while it was a fact of life that the job included all these things.

5. Whose mind must I change to resolve the problem? The committee chairmen, the managers, the coaches, and the parents. No problem with the kids. They just want to play ball.

6. What does that mind think now? They think that the president is responsible for performing all the details of the league.

7. How will I know when the situation is resolved? When we have had a successful year and I have not done one lick of physical work; all the committees are functioning as they should; and no parents contact me to give me a hard time.

ACTION

1. Join the key individuals and the key issues. Traditionally everyone involved in this Little League thinks the president does all the work.

2. Why do they believe this? All the previous presidents have always done all the work.

3. What would it require to separate them from this belief? A president that didn't work and everything still got done, maybe better than before.

4. What is the best method to use in this separation? Get the committees and other officials so involved that they will do their assigned tasks willingly. They have to make a commitment and believe it.

5. How do I implement the method? I have to make myself a solemn promise not to follow up after anyone. Then I have to tell them the way it is going to be and get them to agree and keep it that way.

6. Once it is over, what steps do I take to assure that it will never happen again? <u>If I handle it right, people will be fighting to be president of the league and bask in all that honor without doing any work. Then I will not have to do it again.</u>

Paul reviewed the results of his analysis. It had become clear to him that the committee chairmen were the key men. He had to really turn them on and keep them functioning during the season. How could he do that?

A review of the Laws of Situation Management might provide some insight into that problem.

"Funny," he thought to himself, "I thought these things only applied to business, but I guess all you need are people." He pulled out a clean sheet of paper and started writing his plan:

Law No. 2 says loyalty is a function of appreciation. (That applies here. All I have to do is make sure that the appreciation comes from me. I'll provide some sort of visible recognition for the chairmen and officers. Everyone in baseball wears hats except the front office. We'll get them special baseball caps so that people will know who they are, and we'll recognize their efforts as they occur.)

Law No. 4 says the effectiveness of a program depends upon the amount of participation delegated. (All I have to do is make sure that all the jobs are passed around and that everyone knows what his personal part is all about.)

Law No. 6 says pride goes before all. (I'll threaten them with public exposure if they goof up.)

Law No. 7 says you have to have measurement. (These jobs are all ends in themselves. The equipment is either brought to the game or it isn't. The ball field is either ready or it isn't. We either have sponsors or we don't. That part should be easy.)

Law No. 9 says improvement is the only practical management goal. (We'll have a bigger and better year than ever before.)

Law No. 10 says nobody really listens. (This means that
they will accept my plan at the meeting, but they won't think
I really mean it. I'll have to make examples of some of them
to really prove my point. That goes back to Law No. 6.

At the Wednesday meeting Paul led the discussion of the
various committee tasks. The vice-president would be responsible for the managers and umpires. There were committees for
parent relations, grounds keeping, equipment, statistics, sponsors, awards, and player development. Each committee's specific functions were documented, and dates were set for task
completion.

Paul explained that the detailed duties of the committees
would be printed and sent to each parent and player, so that
they would know who was responsible for what. He also made
the point several times that if the committee didn't do the job,
it was not going to get done. Everyone would know about it.

The parent relations chairman asked: "What do I do when
a mother tells me that her son only got to play two innings
and the manager's son got to play all seven?"

"Tell her," said Paul, "to send her husband over to coach a
team and that then he can play their son all he wants."

At the end of the meeting, Paul presented the special baseball caps. They were bright yellow because he wanted them to
be seen. Everyone seemed pleased and the meeting broke up
in good spirits.

During the next two weeks, the functions of player draft,
sponsor getting, equipment buying, and so forth went off with
relatively few hitches. Everything was on schedule and Paul
was beginning to feel like he had it made. He made a point of
complimenting the committee men on their progress at the
weekly scheduled meeting.

The day before the opening game, Paul walked across the

field and noted that there were some holes in the outfield, that the pitching rubber had not yet been mounted, and that the base lines had been hastily made by pouring dry lime on the dirt. It obviously was not ready for the scheduled double-header to start the season. But he said nothing about it.

The next morning as he escorted the mayor to the mound, before the assembled players and parents, he noted that the field was still in the same shape.

Paul spoke briefly to the mayor who looked a little puzzled, then nodded, and moved off to his car. Paul picked up the megaphone provided for the official ceremony and addressed the quiet crowd.

"I am sorry to say that the game today will have to be canceled because the field is not properly prepared. It would be dangerous to play. The responsibility for preparing the field lies with the grounds committee." He stopped as a waving hand caught his eye. The grounds committee chairman, red-faced, was trying to signal Paul, his eyes begging for mercy.

"However," Paul continued, "I am assured that it will be ready for the second scheduled game which will start at three o'clock. The mayor will be back at that time and will throw out two balls just to make sure."

He never had anymore problems.

The Situation of
the Old Man and the Idea

You're visiting a branch office. The manager is a respected old timer with the company. He's also the president's brother-in-law. He's convinced that your pet project is a bunch of baloney. If you don't sell him, it may well just turn out to be that. What do you do now?

When Alfred Tanner joined the Upperson Company, he immediately recognized that their internal communications system was decrepit, slow, and of course terribly inefficient. Salesmen mailed their reports weekly into each area office where they were carefully sorted, classified, retyped, and sent to the headquarters manufacturing office. After processing, they were dispersed to the plants where the order was filled.

As a result, it sometimes took 6 weeks for an order to

reach the manufacturing line. Customers would be calling the plants to find out what happened to their order before the plant even knew the order had been placed. Sometimes bills, mailed from the area office, reached the customer before the order reached the plant.

However, since the Upperson product was a unique and inexpensive thermoswitch, the customers had to be patient. No other switch could match its cost, reliability, and zero maintenance. They were patient, but not happy.

Tanner sized this up immediately. He set about developing a communications system that permitted the salesmen to telex their orders directly to headquarters in a format that could be instantly routed to the proper plant. This process would eliminate classification activities at the branch offices and permit those offices to concentrate on supervising the salesmen. A great many jobs could be eliminated, but since the company was shorthanded in other areas, the people could be used to fill open requirements. All in all, it looked like a brilliant solution.

The president liked it. He was enthusiastic, so enthusiastic in fact that he gave Alfred an on-the-spot raise. Buoyed by this event, Alfred hardly noticed that he was being directed to prove the system in the field before incorporating it system-wide. It was suggested that he start with the Atlanta office.

Al was half way through lunch with the Atlanta manager, George Webster, before he began to sense that he was in trouble. The older man had met him at the airport, hustled him to the car, and driven him a pleasant 15 miles to the country club. "A little lunch, a fast nine holes of golf, and a chance to get acquainted," George had said. "Always plenty of time for business, and it gets done faster and better when two fellows know each other."

The lunch and game were a delight to Al. George was one of the most knowledgeable and amusing persons he had met. By the time they were relaxing in the locker room, the day was almost over and not one word had been said about the new communications system. It was becoming apparent to Al that he was not going to get the opportunity to discuss it. Each mention of business brought from George short amusing anecdotes on the philosophy of business. The point of each tale being that the young rush themselves to death and accomplish very little. Al decided to wait until the next day.

Upon reporting into the office the next morning, Al was hard put to get some time with George who was continually tied up with customers and salesmen. He worked with Les Pearson, the assistant manager, but soon ran out of things that could be done without agreement from George. Al began to realize that he was being put on. It was apparent that George wanted no part of any kind of change, no matter how efficient it was supposed to be. He would particularly resist any change that did not originate from his own office. Frustration piled upon frustration as Al struggled to search out the required base data from the office personnel. They weren't going to help, at least not willingly. They would answer specific questions, but volunteered nothing. At one point Al picked up the telephone to call headquarters and report the lack of cooperation. Then he realized that he would have nothing to report that would stand up. The assistant manager was at his service and Webster was really tied up. The people were answering his questions. He had had a whole afternoon alone with the branch manager—what more could he want?

He was going to have to pluck this tough old bird himself.

That evening Webster, Pearson, and Al had dinner together. Al forced the conversation around to the new system. He stayed on it until George finally had to admit that he had, indeed, read the recommendations and did indeed consider them worthy. However, he could see no need for rushing into them at this time. Business was good, the customers could be handled, and after all there had been many new men in the company with new ideas over the years and if we had done half of the things they wanted to we'd be bankrupt now." George concluded his discussion with the recommendation that Al get a few more years under his belt in the company, and then they could discuss it some more.

Al pointed out the savings in money, time, and personnel. He noted that the company's controller had agreed that these savings would add up to a dollar value equivalent to 8 percent of sales, and that could become an increase in profit. George wasn't impressed. The dinner broke up on this discordant note, but George did agree to give Al one uninterrupted hour in the morning to "try again."

The very disturbed young man wondered what to do. Why couldn't that idiot see the advantages to the company in this new method? Because it was new? Because it wasn't his? Because he really didn't think it would work? Because he didn't like him?

After some thought Al decided that none of these things were the basic issue. There had to be something else, and he better find it quick. Now he knew why the president had picked this office to start. If you could sell Webster, you could sell anyone. If Webster didn't want to do it, the other managers wouldn't do it either. And for good reasons. George had always had the best producing territory. He always met or exceeded his quota and groomed the executives of the company. He was riding right on top; why should he go for a new scheme like this?

Alone that night in his hotel room, Al decided that he had come to the end of his road. All else having failed, he decided to try a little Situation Analysis.

AWARENESS
1. *What seems to be the situation?*

I can't convince Mr. Webster that my new system would be valuable to him. It doesn't turn him on.

2. *How did I find out that the situation existed?*

I have been listening to him, and there is absolutely no indication that he is going to take it seriously.

3. *What is the potential effect of this matter?*

Obviously, the system will not be installed if I cannot overcome this office. A man who cannot sell a perfectly good idea like this will not be kept around very long.

4. *How serious is it?*

Very serious. It could cost me my job, and it will certainly cost me a lot of self-respect.

5. *How much time do I have to extricate myself?*

Not more than a few days.

EVALUATION

1. *What evidence leads me to believe that the situation exists?*

Personal observation and the spoken words of George Webster.

2. *What is the specific source of this evidence?*

It is all around me. Nothing happens. No one is interested.

3. *Do I know the evidence is factual?*

No doubt at all.

4. *Could I list the steps that created the situation?*

Yes, George is the Duke of Atlanta. He has a genuine success record in the company that gives him a lot of freedom. He has no more company ambitions and no fear. Therefore, he will not do things he genuinely believes in.

5. *Whose mind must I change to resolve the problem?*

George Webster's.

6. *What does that mind think now?*

That this new system will interrupt his orderly life and require him to make changes that he didn't invent.

7. *How will I know when the situation is resolved?*

When the system is installed and working, and I have George's support in putting it through the rest of the company.

ACTION

1. *Join the key individuals and key issues.*

George doesn't want to put the program in because he thinks it isn't going to do *him* any good.

2. *Why does he believe this?*

Because he doesn't have any evidence that it is going to do him any good.

3. *What would it require to separate him from this belief?*

Show him how he could save a lot of time that he could use for his own benefit, or show him how he could gain something.

4. *What is the best method to use in this separation?*

Find out what interests him besides his job, and convince him that he can do both better by using this system.

5. *How do I implement the method?*

First find the other interest, then use salesmanship, and then let him change the system enough that he can take some credit for it.

6. *Once it is over, what steps will I take to assure that it will never happen again?*

I'll make sure that people think they have a problem before I volunteer a solution.

After thinking the thing through, Al took a new tack with the older man. Instead of trying to sell his idea he just listened. For 3 days he listened while George talked about the business, about himself, about the state of the country. Finances did not seem to be a problem to him, so Al discarded the thoughts of bonuses or rewards. George was already one of the big men in the company, and he had no desire to be president.

After much discussion and probing Al finally found a clue —George was very interested in public service. George noted in passing that he had been asked to serve on the State Industrial Commission, an unpaid but vital job and that he was really interested in public service. But he confided to Al that his job just didn't give him time to do it; and he did not feel that it would be fair to the company for him to take early retirement.

This then was the opening. Al pointed out that George could have his cake and eat it too if he could handle his job in less time. They made a rough analysis of how George spent his time, and found that two-thirds of his effort was spent supervising the activities that would be eliminated under the new approach. Suddenly George became interested in the idea and for the first time examined it in detail. He pointed several aspects out to Al that required change or improvement, and the suddenly active Les Pearson helped modify some of the transmission procedures to fit actual practice.

They outlined a seminar to be used in explaining the system to field people and customers. George personally called all the other field managers and told them what a great thing this new system would be.

The system was installed over the next few months; and because of the support given by the field managers, it actually did work and actually did save the time and money that it was supposed to.

Al had learned an important lesson, but as he thought about it he realized that he had already learned it several years ago but had forgotten. He leafed through his personal files and found an essay that had been written some time ago by a friend who was a value analysis specialist.

The chief executive of a company is approached by a corporate staff man with the suggestion that a certain amount of cost could be removed from the products by doing a value analysis engineering study.

Since there is no simple way out of the situation, the chief executive grants permission for the study, and perhaps selects the product to be attacked. Unless he is an unusual person, he will probably pick the most difficult item in his line. The specialist accepts the challenge and goes to work.

Some time later he makes his report and everyone is greatly pleased. Honest savings through process changes, component substitution, work simplification, and other legitimate means are shown to be possible. The changes are implemented. The study is proved to be an unqualified success.

The chief executive is delighted. He congratulates the staff specialist and writes a letter of commendation to the corporation president extolling the depth of the accomplishment. The specialist returns to headquarters secure in the knowledge that he has made a convert and true believer.

Some time goes by and the busy specialist happens to think of that particular accomplishment. He begins to wonder why, in the face of all that success, he has not been requested to return to the company and help them some more.

He calls and hints about it, but is given a polite brushoff. A personal interview reveals that the situation is exactly as it was before; except that they are, if possible, less interested. His activities are remembered as an interesting experiment, nothing else.

Producing a verified list of triumphs in other areas gains him nothing except more vague inaction. He returns home to think and ponder. He has been a victim of 'transient gratefulness.' How come?

If you want to know 'how come,' you must first remove yourself from the big picture and settle down to study the key person in the play: the division chief executive. What makes him so coldhearted that he fails to realize the benefits of staff advice and effort? Advice and effort that even he must admit is freely given and professional.

Well, he doesn't really care about reducing the price of that item. He wants it reduced if possible, of course; but that is not what he is spending his time thinking about and working 16 hours a day for.

What he wants is to be the biggest man in his field. He may have a desire to control the product market prices for his field. He may have all kinds of goals. But whatever it is he wants, you can be sure that he knows it; and only he knows it.

Successful staff work can only happen when effort is guided along the path that will help that chief executive achieve his personal goals.

Don't offer to help reduce product costs only because they can be reduced. Offer to help him meet his goals by helping him reduce costs or whatever it is you do.

Find out his goals—determine how your skills can help him achieve them, and make your work commitment that way. It never fails.

Don't approach the man with solutions until you know what his problem is. He may not be interested in your particular brand of happiness. Remarkable though it may be, he will only let you help him add to his brand.

Anything can be sold to anyone if you can find the correct motivation to present them. The unfortunate part is that the motivation usually has to be original with the person; and since individuals are apparently deep wells of complexity and unfulfillment, you may have to fish to find it.

Alfred Tanner went into this situation blindly and almost blew the whole thing because he was so sure of the worth of his plan that he neglected to evaluate its possible effect on other people. To him the value was so obvious that he was a bit shocked not to receive the key to the city.

It was only after he thought about the people relationships involved that he realized his system had nothing to do with solving the problem. Fortunately, as it turned out, his system did have merit; but the results may have been the same with a less astute program.

He found himself being successfully managed during his stay at the branch office. There seemed to be no way of escaping the friendly net that had skillfully been thrown about him. He was being smothered with cooperation and frustrated by the lack of commitment. He was a man with a solution who could not find the proper way to apply it.

This may occur to any of us, and when we recognize it, the time has come to regroup while planning a new approach. Lesser men might make reference to the fact that the corporate president wanted the program implemented. In that case it probably would have happened but would certainly fail. "I knew it wouldn't work—and it didn't."

The Situation of the Quarrelsome Staff

Your subordinates are continually quarreling among themselves, and as a result, you must participate in all levels of activity and problems. They seem to be drawing further apart. The department is getting further behind. What do you do now?

The manufacturing department of Fortune Industries contained 85 percent of the people and all the profit generation for the company. Essentially Fortune was in the subcontracting business, having no proprietary product of its own. They had a complete metal working operation and an extensive electronic fabrication activity. Larger companies would contract their small lot and specialty jobs for Fortune, usually on a short-term basis. However, the company had earned a reputation for good work and on-time delivery, and so their customers kept them well stocked with orders.

Karl Jansen, the manufacturing director, had recently been promoted to that position, having served as purchasing manager for several years. He was pleased with the opportunity and quite happy that the entire manufacturing staff was staying with him since he had little shop experience. The staff consisted of eight department heads. They supervised a total of 574 people and were considered by the company to be knowledgeable, hard-working professionals. The man Jansen had replaced, Harry Briggs, was now executive vice-president and Jansen's boss. Sometimes Karl wondered why one of the eight department heads had not been moved up when Briggs left.

The eight departments of manufacturing were production control (Jim Baton); machine shop (Henry Rush); sheet metal shop (Al Bensen); electronic fabrication (Tim O'Rilley); electronic assembly (Hans Gerhud); manufacturing engineering (Bob Porter); maintenance (Dave Lyons); and inspection (Hugh Brown). Karl immediately decided to start an analysis of the operation to satisfy himself that the most efficient methods were being used. However, this analysis presented its own problem because there really wasn't anyone available to conduct it. The company had no industrial engineering or operations staff personnel who could be called upon for an evaluation of this magnitude.

Karl rejected the passing thought of asking his boss for assistance, since he was likely to consider this an indication that Karl felt the department had been left in bad shape. He considered calling in consultants, but observed that the company was not in the habit of using them—he did not want to be a pioneer just yet.

After reviewing the resources open to him, Karl decided to use his own managers in evaluating the department. What better analysis could there be than one conducted by the men who ran the shops? He would assign them to teams, and each operation could be evaluated for the common good. His next staff meeting was scheduled for 2 weeks from that date, but having given birth to such a creative solution, he could not bear to wait. He called a meeting for the next day.

His managers were somewhat less than enthusiastic about the proposal. They realized that an analysis of this type should take place, but it was immediately apparent that each felt the need for improvement was in an area other than his own.

In amplification of this feeling, they began to discuss the current requirement of the department. Too many reports, too many meetings, and not enough corrective action by other departments.

The managers began to list the problems of the operations —again each had no trouble in his own area but was beset by inadequate material or services coming from the other. It was a rare demonstration, and Karl was a little terrified by the whole thing. They had been searching for a forum to obtain justice and looked to him to dispense it. He dismissed the meeting on the note that he would look into the situation and attempt to find a solution.

At home that night, Karl lifted the papers from his briefcase and paused for a moment to think of the meeting. Not a very good start. The managers felt no obligation to each other. They welcomed the evaluation idea only because it would, at long last, show the unfairness of the system and services thrust upon them.

He sighed and turned to the mail he had not been able to read that day. Since there was a large stack, he separated it into groups. The groups became:

1. Company policy and procedure notices to be disseminated to his staff.

2. Memos from other departments concerning manufacturing internal operations.

3. Memos to him from his managers concerning problems in other departments and demanding solutions to situations that were interfering with their schedules.

4. Reports from the quality control department indicating that the defect rates were rising and corrective action was not being accomplished.

5. Memos from the sales department detailing customer dissatisfaction and stating concern with schedule attainment.

6. Rough drafts of reports written by his staff for his review and correction prior to issuance.

He struggled through the entire pile and disposed of all the documents. However, he realized that it was now well after midnight and that a similar stack would probably show up the next day. Something had to be done. Pouring a fresh cup of coffee he sat back to review the situation. He must be doing something wrong. He decided to review the problem by utilizing the Situation Analysis guide. Feeling a little silly, he picked up his pencil and began to fill out the form.

AWARENESS

1. What seems to be the situation? My staff is uncooperative with me and with each other. They do not seem to trust one another or have common objectives.

2. How did I find out that the situation existed? I first became aware of it when I suggested a mutual efficiency analysis. Their reaction was very negative.

3. What is the potential effect of this matter? If my department heads will not work together, I am doomed to failure in this job.

4. How serious is it? Critical

5. How much time do I have to extricate myself? Usually a new department head has 3 months before he is held responsible for everything that is happening. I probably have 6 months, but I'll concentrate on fixing it in 3.

EVALUATION

1. What evidence leads me to believe that the situation exists? There are several symptoms: assignments are routinely completed a little late; I must personally edit and revise reports; people are late for meetings; administrative chores are always in arrears; staff meetings are nonproductive; I am involved with a half-dozen fire drills a day; every problem is brought to me; we are behind schedule and no one is to blame; and the managers quarrel with each other.

2. What is the specific source of this evidence? My own observations and the reports of the measuring departments such as finance, quality control, and sales.

3. Do I know that the evidence is factual? Yes. I haven't verified each detail but the indication is overwhelming.

4. Could I list the steps that created the situation? Yes, I think it was the result of management methods used during the years of building up the business. The shop managers never had much responsibility and top management was always available to them. The depth of this practice wasn't visible until now when the business is too big for one man to keep in his pocket.

5. Whose mind must I change to resolve the problem? There are eight minds involved—all of my department heads.

6. What does that mind think now? Right now they think that their world begins and ends at the geographic limits of their department. They feel no responsibility for the overall success of the entire operation.

7. How will I know when the situation is resolved? When the operation is on schedule in all areas and my staff is helping each other to resolve and prevent their problems.

ACTION

1. Join the key individuals and the key issues. My managers think they are responsible for their own department exclusively and that they have no part in the total operation, which they leave to me. They are defensive and negative.

2. Why do they believe this? They have been here a long time and have not been asked to act differently.

3. What would it require to separate them from this belief? I think four things are necessary: first, I must establish a better communication base between them as individuals and myself; second, they need to have a better working relationship; third, we need a mutually developed operations plan; and fourth, we require a measurement and problem action system.

4. What is the best method to use in this separation? Each item would require a different method. For the first one I'll set up individual meetings with them—a half hour per week. We'll stay away from problem talk and try to understand each other as individuals. Guess I'd better write a little sketch of each man, as I see him, in preparation for that. The second item means they need to learn to talk with each other. We can have better staff meetings and problem sessions; but after a month or so, I think we should all sit down and evaluate each other. Three and four should be a direct result of the first two. It would be dangerous to start them before the relationships are straight.

5. How do I implement the method? We'll start out slowly. I'll have a "What's your biggest problem?" meeting in the morning; then we'll start the individual and staff meeting. When they begin to show signs of being interested in each other's problems, we'll move on. Guess I'd better sketch out a schedule.

	Weeks											
	1	2	3	4	5	6	7	8	9	10	11	12
Daily "problem" sessions	x	x	x	x	x	x	x	x	x	x	x	x
Weekly individual sessions			x	x	x	x	x	x	x	x	x	x
Staff meetings	x	x	x	x	x	x	x	x	x	x	x	x
Weekly 20-problem meeting				x	x	x	x	x	x	x	x	x
Self evaluation				x			x				x	x
Group evaluation						x						x
Operations plan								x___x				
Measurement system									x___x			

6. Once it is over what steps do I take to assure that it will never happen again? I'm not sure about this, but I think if we

are really communicating with each other, we will recognize changes as they begin to occur and can alter our plan in order to meet them.

Early next morning Karl called his managers together. He noticed that as they straggled in late each had a good excuse. However, he made no comment. After they were seated Karl greeted them and began to speak:

"This will be a brief meeting. Its purpose is to get us started on a little different system of operating here in manufacturing. I believe that we need to get to know each other better and to know each other's problems. You are all experienced men, and so we should be able to develop a mutual assistance method. To do this we will establish three types of meetings in the department.

"Status meeting. Each morning at 8:15 we will meet for 15 minutes. I will ask each of you one question: 'What's your biggest problem?' You state that problem, and we'll go on to the next man. We won't discuss the problems; we'll just state them. After the meeting you can get together with anyone whose problem is similar to the one you have, or when you feel you can be of assistance.

"Staff Meeting. Each Monday afternoon we will meet from 4 to 5 P.M. to discuss departmental operations and our non-product problems.

"Problem status. Each Wednesday afternoon we will meet from 4 to 5 P.M. to develop and discuss a 20-problem list. I would like the chief inspector to maintain this list and to be responsible for that meeting.

"In addition, I would like to meet individually with you for a half hour every week, so that I can learn more about your operation and your people.

"Since we are all busy, and since we should set a good example for our people, it is imperative that each meeting start and end on time. I obtained a Salvation Army contribution can this morning and I'll put it on the bookcase. Anyone late for a meeting will contribute $1 to the can. If a meeting does not end on time, that is my fault; and so I will contribute. Any questions or discussion?"

Dave Lyons, the maintenance manager, nodded and said, "We already have a lot of meetings, Karl. I'm already scheduled for 22 hours a week. I hate to see us starting some more."

"That is a good point, Dave," said Karl. "I think one of the things we need to accomplish is to evaluate the meetings that occur in manufacturing and assess their purpose and effectiveness." He turned to Hugh Brown, "Hugh, let's make Dave's item number one on the 20-problem list. Nothing is more important in this department than the time of the management talent."

No one had any more items, and so Karl started the "biggest problem" session. Most of the men had to pause and think about it. Lyons said "People." Karl wouldn't accept that; therefore, Lyons switched to "Managers who don't tell me about equipment problems until the unit is a complete disaster." It took a few moments of confusion for Karl to remind everyone that the problems were only to be stated at this time and not discussed. They finally got through the meeting. As the men left, Karl noted that they were at least talking to each other, although there were a few indications of overwarmth in the tones. Hugh Brown, who was the most senior of all the managers, was the last to leave. He paused for a moment at the office door and turned to glance at Karl who was still sitting at his desk. Hugh nodded and gave Karl a slow wink before leaving.

The morning meetings had settled into an acceptable routine by the end of the week. The Salvation Army was $12 richer, and the problem statements were becoming more concise and pertinent. Karl noted that very few were repeated.

The staff meetings on Mondays went fairly well, although it was difficult to keep product problems out of the discussion.

It was almost as difficult to get someone to accept action responsibility for an administrative assignment. Progress seemed slow to Karl but he stuck to his schedule, and in the fourth week began the 20-problem meetings.

Everyone was interested in adding problems to the list, but less interested in accepting responsibility for problem resolution in most cases. Therefore, Karl took the position of assigning each problem to two men—the one whose area was most affected and the one whose area was least affected. That pleased no one, but it was some progress. At the second meeting it was noted that no problems had been removed from the list and that several more were awaiting admission.

Karl reviewed his analysis again, gave himself a pep talk, and decided to enter the self-evaluation phase. His individual talks with the managers had produced some evidence that they too recognized the need to change the existing relationships. They were looking to Karl to accomplish it. Each knew, however, that it would require more than a directive to change people's work habits.

During his individual meetings the next week, Karl handed each manager nine slips of paper explaining that they were identical forms to be used for self-evaluation. He asked the managers to complete one evaluation on themselves and then do one for each other manager, including him. They were to keep their own and place the others in a "personal and confidential" envelope until a special staff meeting which would be held the next Saturday morning at a local hotel. At that time, each man would be given the evaluations written by the other managers. He could then compare these assessments with his own and determine where others viewed him differently than he did.

Karl hastened to explain that no personal embarrassment would be involved since no one would see the evaluations but the person involved. They could ask each other questions about the evaluations if they wanted to.

The men were not quite sure about this development, but they decided to go along with Karl since there didn't really seem to be much choice. The form required ratings on ten different personal characteristics:

NAME OF PERSON BEING EVALUATED _____

DATE _____

Characteristic	*Rating*		
	Poor	*Average*	*Very Good*
Cooperation with others	_____	_____	_____
Ability to listen	_____	_____	_____
Skill in expressing self	_____	_____	_____
Interest in helping others	_____	_____	_____
Communication with subordinates	_____	_____	_____
Ability to solve problems	_____	_____	_____
Ability to prevent problems	_____	_____	_____
Punctuality	_____	_____	_____
Ability to view objectively	_____	_____	_____
Stability of operation	_____	_____	_____

On Saturday morning the nine men arrived at the hotel; following Karl's suggestion, they were dressed informally; but despite his urging, they were not very relaxed. After some coffee and shuffling around, they sat at the big table and started their session, Karl carefully choosing a seat other than the head table. "I will be the chairman for this meeting," he said, "because I'm the only one familiar with the procedure. However, at future meetings we'll pick our own chairman."

Each man was asked to talk about himself for 5 minutes, but with the restriction that no reference should be made to his job career—only his personal activities such as hobbies, interests, birthplace, and so forth. Karl spoke first. By the time the third man had spoken, the group relaxed and became interested in this other side of people they had known for so long. Bob Porter got so involved in talking about his hobby of raising roses that the chairman had to remind him of the time limits. Tim O'Rilley, they discovered, repaired old violins—but had never learned to play one.

When the last man had spoken, Karl passed out the completed evaluation slips. Each man received an envelope with eight evaluations of himself completed by the other managers. In addition, there was a blank one. "If you take a few moments to summarize the totals and enter them on the blank copy, then you'll have one form to deal with," said Karl. "This gives you a broader base of comparison." He went on to explain the rules of the meeting.

"Each of us has evaluated himself according to this format. Now we have this same evaluation completed by those who work with us. The object of the session is to compare the two, noting the differences and then asking for comments on the ones that concern you. For instance, I had rated myself as *very good* on 'ability to listen.' However, five of you rated me average and three poor. Obviously we have different opinions. When my turn comes, I hope you will tell me frankly where you feel I am mistaken.

"We will start from one point around the table with one man, and he can ask questions about himself until he is through. Then, we will move to the next, until everyone has had his time in the barrel. There are just three rules:

1. All comments must be constructive.
2. The questioner may not defend himself
3. Ladies are always present; reporters are not.

"Who wants to start?"

There was a brief silence, then Hugh Brown spoke up. "I'll be first, mainly because I seem to have run across a real conflict on two items. The first is cooperation with others. I always thought I went out of my way to be helpful. Anyone have any comments?"

Another silence.

Henry Rush cleared his throat. "Hugh, I think you're very helpful. In fact the problem probably is that you're too helpful. I don't recall a discussion with you yet that you didn't eventually come around to my way of thinking about whether we could use some defective material or not. What I'm saying is that I think we have to look to inspection to be firm and make us do our job right—sometimes you're too easy."

"But, I have always felt that we should be reasonable."

"No defending" said Tim, smiling.

"Let me tell you the other item that bothered me," asked Hugh, "I think it might have something to do with the first one, although it didn't occur to me before. That one is stability of operation. I have had the feeling that my department is dependable and on time all the time."

"I think that's true, Hugh," remarked Hans, "perhaps the reason you were rated low on that one is that you are not consistent in your standards."

Hugh looked puzzled, "How do you mean?"

"Well, I think an example would be best. I have just found out that some of my foremen are saving parts that aren't quite right until the last of the month. They feel that inspection will accept them during that period; whereas, they wouldn't touch them in the first part of the month."

"You mean that we're tough or loose depending upon the shipping dates?"

"That's about it."

"Well I'll be darned. I think you're right. Let me ask about an item that I wasn't going to bring up because I felt that the raters were absolutely wrong. That is ability to solve problems. I have always considered that my strong suit. May I have some comments on my low rating for solving problems?"

"I think, Hugh," said Dave Lyons, "that most of us are going to wind up with low marks in that category. I'm beginning to get the feeling that we have been solving the same problems for a long time without getting anywhere. That is because we have been working on the symptoms and blaming someone else for the situation. When my turn comes I want to get into that in detail. In your case I have to say that your general approach is to resolve the problems that exist right now, not the ones that will affect tomorrow—only today."

Karl's turn was no. 4; and by the time the discussion got to him, everyone was well into the spirit of the meeting. They really gave it to him on his tendency to brush aside excuses and reasons, but volunteered that perhaps they had not immediately fallen in with his action standards. The discussion became free and easy, and amazingly enough each of them seemed to survive their turn without personal embarrassment or hurt feelings. They had picked up the constructive, friendly manner necessary in such activities.

At the end of the morning Karl asked each man his opinion of the exercise. Their comments indicated that a good start had been made toward opening the channels of honest communication between themselves. A lot of the old barriers had been lifted, and they were aware of the need to be united in a common bond. Hans asked Karl what other things could be undertaken in order to further the process. Karl tossed the question back at the group and was delighted to hear them decide to create a master operating plan for the manufacturing operation. They roughed out a schedule and agreed that it should be complete within the next 3 weeks. The first week was to be spent on a detailed evaluation of existing methods and a determination of weaknesses now existing.

Over the next few months the department gradually rounded into an efficient, on-schedule, problem-solving operation. The meetings became useful, problem lists were reduced, and a feeling of cooperation served as the base for the entire activity. Karl was pleased with the result but began to realize that he had made no provisions for preventing a reoccurrence.

This problem was presented to the staff. Their response was to establish a training program for the next level of management below them to assure that the principles they were developing became part of the entire organization. In addition, they scheduled self-evaluation sessions with their subordinates.

It took some time for the managers to realize that the job of preventing a reoccurrence was a continuing one. But once this became routine, the task became easy. Each year they made out a 2-year operating plan and a 5-year operating plan. These were reviewed in depth by all levels of departmental management and then presented to top management for approval. That way everyone agreed upon the rules of the game. The conformance to that plan established the basis for a measuring system that was fair and accurate. Raises and promotions were given on the basis of meeting objectives, resourcefulness, and effectiveness.

The steps that Karl Jansen took to resolve his problem worked well for him. This does not mean that the same solution will apply to other operations. However, it does mean that by following the Situation Analysis guide it is possible to define the problem down to its base elements.

Karl is a man after my own heart. He did not let the product problems cloud his judgment; he took the time to think it out. As a result, he put his finger directly on the basic problem: people relationships. Many managers would be tempted to blame everything on the staff and launch a campaign to whip them into line or replace them.

I'm sure we have all noted that some executives tend to collect a group of trustworthy men and take them along to each new assignment or company. Certainly this has proven effective many times, but often enough it doesn't. A man's reputation grows quicker and deeper when he uses the material at hand and creates success with it. Probably less than 4 percent of the business people in the world are unusual in terms of intellect and competence combined. These are the people who can identify problems, create solutions to fulfill the need, and implement the solutions while keeping everyone happy. There is no use looking for them through personnel; when they're ready to go to work for you they'll let you know. In the meantime, shape the tools on hand the way Karl did. Once the tools are sharp, and working together, the other problems will be manageable.

Business management lives in a problem-oriented world. If we face this fact, it is only right that we should consider the prevention and solution of problems as an authentic performance measurement. If we use this as a performance measurement, we have to examine the specifics. Obviously it is easy to measure the solution of problems. Yet, it may be dangerous to assume that we know how until we have examined all the aspects. But it is easy to measure the prevention of problems.

This somewhat ambiguous sounding statement has its origin in the fact that most managers are knowledgeable people who carefully manage the news concerning any problem in their area of responsibility. It is impossible to tell the amount of actual effort being put forth on any particular problem by listening to the activity reports of the affected manager. It is not possible to determine the difficulty the problems present by observing the problem-reduction activity.

Therefore, we can only measure solution by results: The problem is gone, forever and ever. It is only possible to measure prevention by seriousness: Good problem preventers only have minor problems.

By what characteristics shall we choose to measure a management team? They should be gauged to accurately record their initial effort, their tradition of involvement, and their success in both preventive and resolution fields. The key points are these:

1. Susceptibility to problem eruption
2. Causes of typical problems
3. Seriousness of typical problems
4. Adeptness at problem identification
5. Skill in problem resolution

Let's take them one by one to examine their meaning and relevancy. If they are to be our key means of measurement, it is essential that we understand their content.

Susceptibility to Problem Eruption

What is their batting average concerning problem activity in the past? Is this a team that always has problems that involve people outside their plant? Do staff experts spend a lot of time there? Are the problems similar? Do they have the same problem several times as it flows through the plant?

Cause of Typical Problems

The cause I mean here is a differentiation between *systematic* problems and *situation* problems. Systematic problems come because the operating program of the team did not permit heading off the problem or finding it early. This type of problem is easily identified because fixing and eliminating it forever involves doing something in an area not directly involved with the problem. It means changing a procedure, an organization, or an operating plan.

Situation problems occur because something outside of the normal control of the team changes.

It is possible to determine who is the most consistent problem contributor by categorizing situations according to organizational responsibility and being completely cruel about it.

Seriousness of Typical Problems

Problems not solved immediately that will vastly affect the schedule, cost, or quality to a significant extent are the type that show the management team to be delinquent in prevention areas. The successful team only has the small worrisome nuisance problems that occur from running a tight shop.

They may lose some sleep for you but will not put you out of business or lose you a valued customer.

The poor team always has "end of the world" problems.

Adeptness at Problem Identification
The high-performance team finds its own problems, identifies them, and solves them. The high-performance team tells the customers and the corporate entity about the problems, instead of vice versa. They have an accurate, dynamic, and topical reporting system that requires assessing the state of their activities on a daily basis. They cannot get too far into the soup without having a sign that something is changing. Planned detection is more important than unplanned.

Skill in Problem Resolution
How long does a problem last? How soon does it, or its brother, come back?

The Situation of
the Unwanted Improvement

Tom Johnson, a staff engineer assigned to the headquarters staff of XYZ Corporation, was called to his boss's office to discuss the Premier Pump situation. Tom had only been in headquarters for 3 months, having been assigned to the electronics-system division for 6 years prior to this move. At electronics he had spent most of his time in acceptance test and material review. Moving to headquarters was a big opportunity for him, and he wanted to do a particularly good job. However, up to this time he had not been given a specific assignment to tackle on his own. Working with the other staff members and going through the orientation program had been interesting, but he was getting anxious to get his teeth into a real problem.

"Tom," said his boss, "I would like you to go out to

Premier Pump and take a look at their overall quality situation. Here is a list of primary items."

1. Premier has been a member of the corporation for one year. It was a family-owned company, and, as a matter of fact, John Selden is still general manager and his brother Ed is chief engineer. They're good men, and we're delighted that they decided to stay with us.

2. Premier is a successful company and is considered the quality leader in their field even though their price is a little above the rest of the market. This folder will give you some information on their organization and the products involved. You'll have to get whatever else you need from them.

3. Your assignment is to determine what steps are required to lower their costs from a quality standpoint, what can be done to eliminate the rising customer complaints about product quality and to get them on a permanent quality improvement program. The most important aspect is the cost of quality. As you know, cost of quality is the expense of waste: how much it costs the company for rework, scrap, inspection, test, warranty, field service, etc. For many companies, it runs as high as 15 percent of sales; but we know from our experience that it doesn't need to be any more than 4 percent of sales. The amount saved becomes profit.

4. Take all the time you need but keep me informed daily, with a short note, of your problems and progress. I won't communicate with you unless you specifically request it. You shouldn't need any more than 2 weeks, but make sure that any plans you feel need to be implemented get implemented and stay implemented.

5. Our corporate policy is to permit the divisions to run their own affairs as long as they are making money. That means that whatever you get them to do will have to be done because it is right, not because it is directed.

Tom took the folder and returned to his office. Looking it over, he learned that Premier had sales of 30 million dollars a year; returned 4.8 percent after taxes; had 1,800 employees; and produced a varied line of fractional horsepower pumps that moved water, oil, milk, and about anything that was liquid.

Their primary customers were original equipment manufacturers, but they sold about 20 percent of their product to distributors and repairmen as replacements.

Their share of the market had been running a consistent 38 percent over the years. They had dropped to 32 percent in the past years although their sales held up due to the increased market available. They were still the largest in their field.

An organization chart was attached:

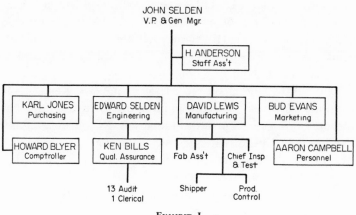

Exhibit I

Tom called John Selden for an appointment and was assured of an enthusiastic welcome.

"We're always interested in improving our quality and will be glad to get some expert help. Of course we can't afford to spend too much on it like they do in the space business, but I think you'll be pleased with what we are doing. Ken Bills, our quality assurance manager, will meet you at the airport to make sure you can find the plant and get settled at the motel.

I'll plan on seeing you when you get to the plant tomorrow."

Ken Bills did meet Tom at the airport, and Tom was immediately impressed by Ken's energy and obvious interest in his job. He had been with Premier for 12 years, 6 as quality assurance manager. He belonged to the quality technical societies and was very active in those circles. He told Tom about his operation as they drove to the plant.

"Under our setup, manufacturing does the inspection and we evaluate their results. I have 14 people. We run inspections and tests after manufacturing, using samples, and continually audit the product. When we find something wrong, we investigate it and then go back to manufacturing or engineering to get it fixed. We put quality assurance in the engineering department; so that it could be free of obligation to schedule or cost considerations. Of course, we try to be reasonable and keep the line moving. If we can't sell pumps, we don't have a job."

Tom asked about rejection rates.

"We have some good records on that," said Ken. "We're running 2.5 percent defective in receiving, 6.1 percent in fabrication shops, and 4.2 percent in final test. I know those figures because I had to brief the boss this morning. Usually we just supply monthly reports to each department head, and they discuss them at the staff meetings."

"Are those the results of manufacturing inspection and test or your results?" asked Tom.

"Those are our results. When defects are found in the production operation, the foreman has them fixed. We feel that it is uneconomical to try to keep track of those. However, the foreman records the rework charges and I assess all the scrap costs. We have a good feel. When we get to my office, I'll show you those figures."

The plant was a modern facility, only 2 years old. Premier had moved into it a year before selling out to XYZ. The parking lots were large, and Ken pulled into a spot with his name on it. They walked into the lobby, and Tom was given a badge to wear that said "Visitor, Tom Johnson, XYZ headquarters."

"You can go anywhere you want with this badge. John wanted to make sure that you had all the freedom you wanted."

"Might as well wear a neon sign," thought Tom.

After introducing Tom to John Selden, the general manager, Ken excused himself, promising to be available whenever Tom wanted to start his plant tour.

Selden, a brisk, pleasant man, immediately put Tom at ease. After some small talk they got around to the subject at hand.

"I know your primary concern is our quality costs, and we would appreciate any help we can get along that line. However, most quality control guys only want to put in more checks and safeguards—that runs the costs up more. We're in a commercial business. Now, I always back my quality control guys when they get into it with production—even when I think they're being unreasonable. That's because I want to make sure that our products are good. But if we get too involved, we're liable to inspect ourselves right out of business. Incidentally, I hope you can limit this particular evaluation to 4 or 5 days. This is the busiest part of our year."

Tom asked Selden if there was anything in particular that he could do for him while in the plant.

John got up and closed the door.

"There is one thing. I don't really know much about the quality business, and I'd appreciate your evaluation of Ken Bills's job performance. He's a good engineer, and I can always put him back into design if he's not the right man for the job."

"What specific things would you like me to look for?"

"My greatest concern is that the other managers don't seem to have a great deal of respect for his decisions. We must get into four or five hassles a month on whether or not something is good enough. I'd like to know why he can't handle these things."

Tom assured John that he would look into it and would plan to meet with him in 5 days to provide his initial impressions of the total operation, as well as to offer some recommendations for improvement. He showed the general manager the basic review format for evaluating a company's overall quality operation and told him that he would provide a complete report in that format for future reference.

His primary report, however, would be a list of specific recommendations for improvement (if there were any) and the backup information showing why these items had been selected and pointing out implementation steps as well as potential savings. John would have the opportunity to review the report in detail with Tom before it was submitted to headquarters. Any comments that the general manager had would be included. Tom also pointed out that he must send a daily status report to his boss at headquarters, and asked if John would like to read it before it went out.

"Only if you're talking numbers. We like to make sure that all dollar figures are checked with the comptroller and people figures with personnel before they go to XYZ. Sometimes they get excited up there."

They shook hands after John had firmly told Tom that he was welcome to come see him at any time during his visit. Bills was summoned, and he led Tom back to his office. Since it was late, they agreed to start the next morning, and Tom was driven back to his motel.

The next morning Tom rented a car and drove to the plant. He met Ken Bills in his office.

"Where would you like to start?" asked Ken.

Tom thought a bit.

"I've worked out a kind of plan, Ken. It seems to me that I should get a general understanding of your operation before we begin to get specific. Perhaps we could go over the company in terms of number and types of people and how the quality control department works, and then go on a tour of the plant so I can become familiar with your product. Then we can look at the charts you have and examine some specific problems. Let me ask you a question on that: What do you feel is your biggest problem?"

"I think my biggest problem is trying to get the manufacturing people to understand the need for high quality in our product. In fact that's a problem with all areas. We use a lot of castings for instance, and they're always off dimension. Purchasing says that's as good as they can get for the price we can pay. Manufacturing goes along with them and plans the machining operations to accommodate the defects. The final product works OK but it takes a lot of special checking. Then, too, when we audit the product lines and find something out of specification, they won't change anything. They just figure out a way to use it. Of course that's not all bad; it does keep the product moving."

"What does top management say about these items?" Ken wondered.

"They don't particularly like it but they have to go along, after all we're in a commercial business. My boss feels we write too much down now anyway. That's why he won't issue a casting specification. We do much better giving the foundries the drawing for the final item and then working with them until they come up with a satisfactory unit."

When Tom asked about the number of people, Ken took him over to the personnel department where Tom met Aaron Campbell. They discussed the personnel distribution, and Aaron presented Tom with a chart showing departmental distribution (Exhibit II). He suggested that Tom talk with the individual department managers concerning personnel usage.

Tom asked Aaron what his biggest problem was.

"Guess it would have to be the union. We've only had a

union for 2 years. It started just about the time we moved to this plant. Before that we never had any trouble. But you know the kind oı workers you get today. They're only interested in money, and don't really care about their work. We get 20, maybe 25, grievances a week. Usually they wind up being nothing but a lot of hot air. It's hard to make these people understand who owns the plant. But that's not the kind of stuff that interests you quality types. If I can do anything for you during your stay, please let me know."

Tom and Ken proceeded through the plant. It was generally very well laid out; and Tom, for his purposes, mentally divided it into three areas: receiving and stockrooms; metalworking fabrication; and final assembly. All areas were well-lighted, and people seemed to be working steadily. They had an adequate amount of room. Housekeeping—except for the fabrication shop—was also adequate. As Ken said, "You can't expect a machine shop to look like someone's living room."

EXHIBIT II

Total Personnel—1,782	
Manufacturing, direct labor *	1,187
indirect labor	214
Engineering	197
Purchasing	32
Personnel and labor relations	27
Marketing	67
Quality assurance	15
Labs (mechanical research)	11
General management & clerical overhead	32
	1,782

* Includes 173 inspection & test personnel.

The Receiving Area

All incoming material arrived by truck and was placed in a receiving bay. Production control people sorted the lots as they arrived and assigned a priority to them. This was done with red, amber, and green stickers. Red had the highest priority. After the lots had been logged, they were moved to the inspection area. Expeditors with shortage lists moved the lots to the inspectors in order to assure that the highest priority items were handled first.

Inspection equipment was not complex—mostly mechanical gages—and seemed to be in good order. The inspectors seemed to know their jobs. Ken said that most of them had been there for a good while and knew the parts so well that it wasn't necessary to maintain a lot of records. If they needed a print, it could be obtained from engineering in a few moments.

An average of 60 lots was received each day. The 6 inspectors and 1 tester could process about 50 a day. The difference was made up by working regular overtime.

The stock rooms were enclosed in wire cages, and all material was distributed by the production control personnel. Raw material was particularly protected. It had to be issued in the presence of one of the receiving inspectors to make sure that the wrong material was not put out.

Ken handed Tom a chart showing the receiving rejection rate for the past year. "As you asked me before, this represents the findings by my man over there. He checks some of the lots going into stores on a sample basis."

"What does he do when he finds one wrong?" asked Tom.

"Let's talk to him about that."

The audit inspector explained that he selected parts at random as they came through and checked them against the purchase order and drawings to determine how well the inspectors had done. "When I find one wrong, I send it back to the inspector, and he checks it again. Then it goes to stock. Mostly I check the amber and green sticker boxes. The red are hand-carried to the line, and line inspectors there can cover it."

"Do you keep a list of the rejections against each inspector? And if so, what do you do with it?"

The audit inspector stated that he did keep such a list and

supplied it to the receiving supervisor daily. He didn't know what the receiving supervisor did with it but assumed that it was used to rate the inspectors.

As they walked away, Tom asked Ken what happened to material rejected in the receiving inspection area and how much of that there was.

"Couldn't be very much. We only send two or three lots a month back to the suppliers. When something doesn't check out the inspector gets together with the expeditor, and they bring a manufacturing man over to see if he can use it. Sometimes they get a buyer or engineer on it too. These are very aggressive, dedicated guys, and they are quite inventive. We don't have much difficulty here. Wait until we get into assembly. They're the problem area."

Before going into the manufacturing areas, Ken introduced Tom to the manufacturing manager, Dave Lewis. Although Lewis appeared to be a real bull-of-the-woods type, Tom found him to be extremely practical and quite concerned about the product quality.

"My scrap and rework figures are quite low for this type of industry, I think. Yet we are still spending too much money. Last month I spent $2,480 on rework alone. That is the equivalent of five people—a lot of money. My scrap was $7,000."

"Do you always use the same people for rework?" asked Tom.

"In some cases we do, particularly in final assembly; it takes a real fine hand to put some of these parts together if they're a little out of dimension. The rework I was speaking of was that done by the nonrework personnel. We don't count our repair stations as rework; they're a fact of life in every company."

"You have to be practical on these things," said Ken. "If we included the planned rework in our figures each period, they would look real high. How many people are involved here, Dave?"

"In fabrication we have 12 rework people, and in final assembly around 22. Of course, testers are expected to do some adjustment if they have a problem, but that doesn't include disassembly. We're laying out a new pump line, and I'm putting rework stations in three places to speed up the flow. Right now, with our present setup, we have to move the parts on and off the line."

Dave volunteered to be available whenever Tom wanted to see him.

The Fabrication Shop

Ken gave Tom the rejection data for the fabrication shop.

"We kept the data generated by manufacturing inspection for a long time, and we found that it generally ran about twice that picked up by audit. Eventually we got enough confidence in that ratio to just use the audit numbers. I think we're on an improving trend."

The shop consisted of lathes, screw machines, and the usual satellite equipment. Inspection areas were set up in each section, and completed lots were moved to these areas. In addition, the machine operators checked the pieces as they went along. The audit inspectors would select some lots after inspection had been complete and reexamine them. The inspector carried or carted the lots to his own area for this audit.

Repeating the same method as in the receiving area, Tom asked the inspector to explain the procedure. Here the offending inspector was called to the audit area and shown the defects overlooked. Methods of inspection were compared and an agreement reached about why the error had occurred. The lot was then sent to the rework area, unless it was on the critical shortage list. Then the expeditor was called, and he arranged a meeting to accept the material.

The purchasing manager, Karl Jones, found that he and

Tom had several mutual friends. Karl was new with Premier, having joined them less than a year ago.

"This business is sure different than Aerospace," said Karl. "Here you buy on price and delivery exclusively. You've a lot more room in the tolerances, and you don't have to live with those high-quality products. Of course, we insist that the suppliers meet the requirements; if we didn't they'd send us junk. But where we used to have a specification an inch thick for every little detail, now we just get outline drawings, and our buyers can use a little more judgment. However, since I'm the one that gets the devil if the parts aren't right, we're very careful on this quality thing. Ken here has a screaming fit with me at least twice a week, and I think that we're beginning to go more his way.

"I get reports from his guys in receiving inspection, and we try to take action on them. However, in most cases the error is missed inspection—not much we can do about that."

"How do you pick your suppliers?" asked Tom.

That's another advantage of the commercial business. We just write up the orders and the salesmen come in here everyday. We can give the same package to two or three outfits and wait for their bids. Of course, if we have a bad experience, we don't have to go with them again. Ken has sat in on a couple of those bid conferences."

"I don't envy you those conferences," said Ken, "I'll stick to the quality business."

Final Assembly

The purchased and fabricated parts came together in the assembly area. Production control people delivered the various parts to the end of each line where they were transferred to bins. Assembly personnel did their portion of the work and then laid the unit on a conveyer belt to carry it to the next operation. After the fabrication shop, it seemed well ordered and quiet. Tom noticed that everyone wore white coats except the foremen and inspectors. The foremen wore blue coats and the inspectors red. Audit people wore blue.

"As the units come down the line they are given a visual inspection at the end. Then they are placed on the cross room belt and delivered to the test room. It's through this door."

Ken led Tom into a large dust-free area, through an air lock.

The people working in this room were covered from head to foot in white and wore lint-free gloves. Twelve benches were set up on one side and eight on the other.

"These 12 are production testing operations," said Ken. "My main audit effort is on the other side. My 8 people do a 100 percent test of all units before they leave. It is the same test that production does but without the adjustments. That's why they can do it faster."

Since time was getting short, Tom suggested that they go directly to the engineering office and that perhaps they could discuss corrective action at the same time.

Ken introduced Tom to Ed Selden, the engineering manager and Ken's boss. Ed was very agreeable and freely discussed his operation with Tom. In answer to Tom's question about drawing control, Ed replied that this was vested in the individual project engineers.

"They are the ones who have to live and die with the product," said Ed, "so we give them the tools to do the job. That's one thing you'll find here. When we ask a man to do the job, we give him the tools. That's why we give the inspectors to the foremen. It works out much better that way."

Ken discussed the corrective action system.

"Corrective action is centered around the product engineer. Each foreman or inspector has ready access to the product engineer. If it's out of his area, like in purchasing or quality, the product engineer refers it to the proper department. In addition, my staff selects the problems they see, and this is placed on a monthly report to all managers by Ed. Anyone who doesn't take action with the first report, gets clobbered on the second. It's been very effective."

As they talked, Tom received a call from the general manager. John had to leave for Los Angeles at noon the next day and would be gone for a week. He wondered if Tom was well enough along to discuss his findings the next morning, and if so, would Tom mind if the staff was invited to participate. Tom agreed.

Two days later Tom was back in headquarters sheepishly admitting that his trip had been a failure.

Retrospect

It must be apparent to anyone who has had anything to do with a manufacturing operation that Premier management runs a sloppy shop and that their controls are nonexistent. In his meeting with the staff, Tom Johnson pointed out that rejection rates were incomplete and biased; inspection, testing, and rework were all excessive; some drawing control must be exercised; the quality manager could do with higher personal standards; and many, many other things. So many items of improvement were available that Tom got carried away.

Selden and his team were very upset with his suggestions and closed their ears to such criticism coming from a mere boy. The meeting, held to explain his findings, became quite cool in a hurry, and Tom returned to headquarters frustrated with his failure.

He deserved what happened to him. He worked diligently at detecting and listing the details that must be corrected. However, he did this on the unwarranted assumption that the Premier management wanted to correct such deficiencies. Nothing could be farther from the truth. They have no desire to improve. They didn't ask him to come. They think everything's just great. Once the market recovers, they will be right back up there on top again.

You know that's not going to happen, Tom knows it, and

so does everyone but the men that count. Therefore, they must be made to see that they can obtain instant rewards now, in their own operation, without waiting for the fickle market-place or the good fairy.

What measurable items interest them? In this case profit is the only thing. Their profit is not very high and is slipping fast. Tom should have asked himself what he could do to increase that profit before attempting to "sell" his program.

He should have calculated the cost of doing things wrong, the method his boss suggested. If you add up the expenses involved in inspection, test, quality control, rework, scrap, and warranty (and they probably are not including half of it), you will arrive at a figure that represents close to 10 percent of the sales dollar. The actual figures probably would bring it out at 15 percent.

Tom knew that these costs should run only 4 percent of sales. The difference between these figures is attractive enough to get anyone's attention. There is little or no difficulty in attaining these cost levels, and probably improving the product conformance in the bargain.

If, by chance, these should be super-hardheads, Tom still has the option of returning home to state that he offered them a chance to pick up 1.5 to 3 million dollars, and let his boss go into the Situation Management business.

Too many staff people fail in their activities because they try to sell the incidental instead of the prime item. Anything can be measured if you are willing to think about it for a while.

Here is what Tom should have done prior to the meeting:

SITUATION ANALYSIS GUIDE

AWARENESS

1. What seems to be the situation? Premier Pump Management runs a very ineffective operation, yet they are not inter-

ested in improvement. If I can't get them to improve, I am in trouble.

2. How did I find out that the situation existed? After spending several days in their plant and meeting their management people, it became apparent to me that this was the case.

3. What is the potential effect of this matter? This is my first big assignment, if I fail, there may be no more. I will be back in a plant, somewhere, doing time studies.

4. How serious is it? Critical.

5. How much time do I have to extricate myself? The meeting will be tomorrow morning. I only have a few hours.

EVALUATION

1. What evidence leads me to believe that the situation exists? The management is shipment-oriented. They don't really care about quality; inspection only checks items that are not needed at the moment: Housekeeping is terrible; the personnel guy thinks people are no damn good; the quality control manager is weak. Their quality costs are not calculated, but if you add up the people and costs involved, just roughly, it is at least 11 percent of sales.

2. What is the specific source of this evidence? My own observations while being carefully guided around the plant. Heaven knows what is really going on that I didn't see.

3. Do I know that the evidence is factual? Yes, I have seen and witnessed it myself.

4. Could I list the steps that created the situation? This was a family-owned company with a unique product and no competition. The customers had to take what they got. Over the years, competition set in; and their share of the market began to diminish. However, they did nothing to reduce their costs or improve their product. The world is passing them by.

5. Whose mind must I change to resolve the problem? John Selden's first of all, but the entire management team thinks the same way.

6. What does that mind think now? They think that if they go on the way they have, the market will change and they will get back their share, perhaps with a price increase. They also think their operating method is just grand.

7. How will I know when the situation is resolved? When they accept a list of the improvements I think are necessary and set about doing them enthusiastically, even to the point of adding some of their own.

ACTION

1. Join the key individuals and the key issues. The management doesn't think they need to improve.

2. Why do they believe this? They have seen no evidence that it is in their interests to change their style of operating.

3. What would it require to separate them from this belief? Some specific evidence that if they change their ways, their results will be dramatically better.

4. What is the best method to use in this separation? The only thing I have going for me is the calculation that they are spending 11 percent of sales for the cost of quality instead of the 4 percent we know is possible. The difference is 1.8 million bucks.

5. How do I implement the method? I forget all of the other things I have to tell them about their operation and give the cost to them straight. If they are not interested, then I'll let my boss do it.

6. Once it is over what steps do I take to assure that it will never happen again? I'll help them install a better cost-report-system, so that they won't get so far off the track again.

Situation Prevention Guide

1. What are the short- and long-range purposes of this action?
_____
_____
_____
_____
_____
_____
_____
_____
_____
_____

2. Have I prepared the way for the successful completion of this action by establishing communications and coordination with those who will be affected? _____
_____

_____
_____
_____
_____
_____
_____
_____
_____
_____
_____

3. Is the implementation method I have chosen the result of a thoughtful situation analysis, including "best" and "worst" case anticipated results, or am I following normal practices?

_____
_____
_____
_____
_____
_____
_____
_____
_____

The ABC's
of Situation Prevention

*7*he folklores of all nations have at least one thing in common: they are well-stocked with adages designed to pass on wisdom accrued by the experience of living. Most of these refer to the prevention:

> "A stitch in time saves nine."
>
> "Marry in haste, repent at leisure."
>
> "The more things change, the more they remain the same."
>
> "Those who marry for money earn every cent."
>
> "Those who cannot remember the past are condemned to repeat it."
>
> "As the twig is bent so grows the child."
>
> "A wise man builds his house on a rock."

The list goes on; everyone has his favorite. You may note that although the sayings are repeated often, and solemnly, the person doing so doesn't feel they apply to him. They're for other people.

That is what makes situation prevention so difficult—The rules don't apply to us. When we considering marrying in haste, we justify our decision by another adage: "Love conquers all." If we decide not to take a stitch at this particular time, we quote: "Don't tarry, tomorrow is here."

It will do little good to follow the rest of this particular thought unless we can convince ourselves that the procedures for staying out of trouble, by systematically preventing it, apply to us personally. We are inclined to feel that others impose situations upon us rather than we being the creators of our own difficulties.

The modern-day equivalent of avoiding a "stitch in time" can be found in every business, be it a real estate office, a grocery store, or a manufacturing plant. The inevitability can be noticed when a manager sighs from the fatigue of strain and worry and mutters, "We never have time to do things right, but we always have time to fix them." Certainly an astute observation. Unfortunately, he doesn't really believe it, because he doesn't try to change it. He thinks that the next program will be different, and so he doesn't examine the past errors to determine where he began to go wrong. He is really saying that he doesn't take time to prevent problems.

We must make some attempt to change this feeling instead of looking at prevention as an emotional item of judgment. Let's try to put it in a cold nonpersonal text: *Prevention is planned anticipation.* (This should not be confused with being a worry wart.) We can *anticipate* without becoming emotionally involved.

Probably the most dramatic application of planned anticipation is the system-management technique used in the space- and weapon-system industry (systems used only because the customer absolutely demanded them). Apollo scientists worked out every detailed step necessary to get to the moon and back long before the first piece of hardware involved was developed. Each step, measured in microseconds, was then examined for its content and for its effect on the next step (as well as the total system), and then given to a group to develop. All known or anticipated problems were identified and resolved before the system was committed.

Very few of us have the resources available to conduct complete system-management analysis or to construct a computerized PERT chart before we move out on our normal actions. However, it is possible to train ourselves to use the computer in our heads and peer into the future effect of our planned actions in order to see what might happen. We do some of it anyway. Most often we don't. Have you ever:

Run out of gasoline?

Bought something that turned out to be worthless?

Missed a plane?

Had a customer return an item because it didn't function properly?

Burned a dinner?

Driven 60 miles out of your way?

Lost a girl friend?

Been involved in an accident?

Been surprised by what someone thought?

Paid too much interest?

Most of us have done these things. Most of us will agree that they could have been prevented if we had taken a moment to review our program before acting. Consumer bureaus state that very few people are swindled if they resist the opportunity to "buy now because the offer expires at midnight."

What is the logical extension of the action of planned anticipation? It is anticipating potential disaster on a routine basis, preferably by following a quick procedure of evaluation.

Situation-prevention logic is keyed by three questions. If

each is considered for but a microsecond prior to commitment, the chance of problem avoidance is good. If each is considered for a total of 30 seconds, the probability of avoidance is excellent. A concentration for 2 minutes guarantees results.

These questions are.

1. What are the short- and long-range purposes of this action?

2. Have I prepared the way for the successful completion of this action by establishing communications and coordination with those who will be affected?

3. Is the implementation method I have chosen the result of a thoughtful situation analysis, including "best" and "worst" case anticipated results, or am I following normal practices?

Let's take a simple everyday case as an example. You are driving down a six-lane freeway in the fast, or inside, lane. All lanes are crowded but the traffic is moving in an orderly fashion. You are alert and attentive to the driving job since you must turn off within the next few miles.

The warning sign for your turnoff appears overhead and states that you must leave the highway from the far right-hand lane in 2 miles. That means a six-lane change. It is time to start moving over. You flash your signal light and look for room in the next lane in order to work across.

1. The immediate purpose of your action is to place yourself in a position to exit from the highway at the proper exit. Your long-range purpose is to get to your final destination safely.

2. You have opened communications with the other drivers affected, by flashing your signal light in order to indicate your desire to change lanes. However, you recognize that it is strictly a one-way communication since you have no way of knowing their willingness to permit you to do this. Therefore, as you cross, you must carefully try to evaluate the intentions of each driver around you.

3. This exit was chosen by you before you ever got on the highway. If you've never traveled that way, the selection may have been made by a friend. But you feel you're stuck with it. The best thing that can happen is that you successfully cross the six lanes in the 2 minutes, or less, allocated. The worst is that you may be involved in an accident that will exterminate you, and several others, right there on the spot. In between these two "cases" lie two options: going to the next exit (and being late), or forgetting the whole thing (the coward's way).

The important analysis in this case is the comparison between the reward for success and the penalty for failure. They are too far apart. It may be better to consider moving to the next exit and circling back, with its resultant loss in time, than to be a stubborn planner and force your way to the exit in a too short-time frame. Your next trip will be easier because you will know that you must be in a right-hand lane earlier than you anticipated.

The value of these questions lies in forcing ourselves to review our thinking and opportunities in a routine fashion in order to avoid an illogical act. Consideration-time span is relatively short, once the meaning and usefulness of the considerations are clear. Let's examine them in greater depth by using the *Situation Prevention guide.*

1. *What are the short- and long-range purposes of this action?*

Everyone seems to have his own definition of the intent of PURPOSE. (I have placed it in capital letters because that is the way it seems to be viewed, as some noble abstract or spiritual sort of thing. Disraeli said: "The secret of success is constancy to purpose." Shakespeare reported: "The flighty purpose never is o'ertook unless the deed go with it." Carlyle laid it out in lifetime terms: "The man without a purpose is like a ship without a rudder—a waif, a nothing, a no man. Have a purpose in life and, having it, throw such strength, of mind and muscle into your work as God has given you."

Everyone has some purpose in life, something he wants to

accomplish, something he believes in—whether he can clearly state it or not—but that does not enter into this discussion. Lifetime purposes should be used for the guidance of conscience and habit. The kind of purpose we are considering refers to the specific task at hand and its objectives. We are concerned with: Why do you want to do this? What do you want to get out of it? How well did you plan it?

Much of the wasted effort in human activity is a result of a lack of clear definition of the *real*, or total, reason for doing something. If you cannot determine why you are doing something, you probably won't do it very well.

In stating the real purpose you must be specifically honest with yourself—no one else needs to know. If you ask a groom the purpose of his wedding, he will tell you about responsibility, lifetime companionship, settling down, and other things —none of which brought him to the altar. His bride could tell you.

If you ask a business manager why he is expanding a certain function, he will talk about reducing exposure, increasing profitability, and moving into new markets. His real purpose may be to make vice-president.

Don't miss the opportunity to expose your real purpose to yourself.

2. *Have I prepared the way for the successful completion of this action by establishing positive communications and coordination with those who will be affected?*

("But Orville, I thought *you* were going to put the gasoline in the engine.")

In game or war situations, it is considered proper to keep the competition from knowing the purpose of your program. As a result, it is sometimes not possible to tell your own people.

In matters of high-corporate strategy a similar situation may present itself. Some corporations are more secretive than the Armed Forces, in this day of mergers and competitition.

Unfortunately, they sometimes exaggerate the depth of the "competition" and don't tell anyone.

In the normal business and personal situations we face, it is vital to share our scheme with those who will be affected by it (and therefore will find out anyway). The amount of active interest a person takes in another's plans is proportional to how early in their execution or development he becomes part of the process. (Law No. 4) Active interest usually means help, or at least lack of nonhelp; so it is a vital thing to stimulate.

To communicate properly you must, of course, know what you are doing, or plan to do. Then you must be able to state this purpose in a way that those involved will be able to understand. After this, you must develop a measurement method that is not unacceptable and that can be used to let people determine progress.

But all these things are of little use unless you can deter mine with whom you want to communicate, what you want them to know, and what you want them to do about it.

This one item has to be the biggest problem in the communications activity. You have to be very careful to determine who can positively or adversely affect your operation, even though it might be by doing nothing. History is full of stories where a little nameless, faceless man who wasn't informed or considered caused the fall of the mighty. The mishap of the nail that held the horseshoe, or didn't hold the horseshoe, probably occurred because no one told the blacksmith that this was an important horse; and he was relying on warranty and the laws of probability to guarantee his reputation.

If you plan to do something, you must consider the effect it will have on others. Not only the others who appear on the organization chart but those who will be affected. And you must pass the information to them in a context that appeals to their interest.

Many a plant manager has busily announced: "Parking lot No. 3 will be closed for 6 weeks," only to find that his people interpreted this to mean that the third shift was going to be laid off. After all, that's where they normally park. What he was really trying to say was: "While parking lot No. 3 is being repaved, it will be closed for 6 weeks."

If you've ever returned from vacation to find newspapers piled waist-high in front of your door, you can recognize that you forgot to include someone in on your plans. You can ask yourself why the newspaper boy didn't stop when it became apparent that no one was home. He didn't stop because he was hurt by not being told, and he would rather create customer dissatisfaction than lose his pride and manhood. (Law No. 6)

Pride and manhood or womanhood: That is the item you must be concerned with when determining *who*. Almost every conflict of man throughout the years has been caused by real or implied impugning of pride or manhood. Pride is probably the most predominate reason. No one can stand to be ignored. Everyone wants part of the action.

Whose pride would be affected by your project?

Let's suppose that Sam is the owner of a clothing store. Business is fairly good, but not good enough. He needs a little something to spur things on; hence, he decides that he will issue gold-plated charge cards to the significant people in his community. This, he thinks, will make them very conscious of the store's presence and the respect in which their patronage is held. A list of prestige people is prepared, and cards are disbursed by the advertising agency. Then he sits back and anticipates the profits.

The next thing you know business is off. Not only is business off but the clerks are snarly; the credit manager is having a snit; and some of his oldest customers are giving Sam the cold shoulder. How could this happen to such good intentions? Why should these people be acting so strangely. Poor Sam!

The clerks are upset because he didn't give them the

chance to put some of their valued, but lower-class, personal customers on the list for this status symbol; the credit manager is unhappy because he didn't get to run the credit checks and issue the cards (he knows Sam will hold him responsible for any delinquent accounts that might result); and his old customers are upset because Sam obviously took them for granted and did not include them in the new feature.

Test: Select one reaction that isn't a function of pride.

The age of unilateral action is past. There are no "all-powerful" managers any more. There is very little that even the most determined man can accomplish by himself. Even the assassin must have a victim.

In selecting the "who" you must consciously determine a list of those whose pride could be affected by the action. You can think in groups, if you are so inclined, but you must be careful not to omit anyone. For instance:

Harvey Stockton was elected to his state legislature at the age of twenty-four, the youngest man ever to accomplish that feat. He was personable, articulate, energetic, intelligent and well-educated and obviously had a great future before him. Some people were already concerned that the state constitution required the governor to be at least thirty years old. Harvey was approached by several lobbyists with discrete offers of large returns for minimal effort. He sent them scurrying, and in one case, personally arrested the man and turned him in to the state attorney general.

One day, a group of chicken farmers approached Harvey concerning the lack of a sufficient bounty on chicken hawks. Because no one actively pursued these birds in order to collect the meager bounty they were multiplying rapidly and destroying chickens at a record rate throughout the State. The farmers showed Harvey figures to prove their point.

He was irate and immediately dropped a bill into the hopper to raise the bounty. He made a stirring speech in the legislature in favor of the bill. The increased bounty was soundly defeated, and along with it his chance of future political achievement. It seems that the hawks really weren't that active. As a matter of fact, the bird conservation club (whose membership consisted of every major industrialist and politician in the state) was desperately trying to find a way to save the species. They did not reflect too happily on the judgment of the new legislator. Soon even the lobbyists were not speaking to him.

3. Is the implementation method I have chosen the result of a thoughtful situation analysis, including "best" and "worst" case anticipated results, or am I following normal practices?

The more creative you are in conceiving new situations, the more you must attend to the danger of using the accepted or normal approach. New ideas require new implementation methods. They require an estimate of total reaction. Rousseau entered into a literary discussion of the rights of man. His purpose was to question the thinking of the French Academy. His result was to incite the French Revolution. Luther wanted more say about church policy given to the local level. His result was a bifurcation of the existing church.

Whether these happenings were good or bad in their total effect has nothing to do with our discussion. What really matters is that neither man got what he had planned and, in effect, created a happening beyond his power to control.

The pragmatist regards each new device from the standpoint of "What does it do?" By this method he reduces everything to its mechanical use and then can judge its worth on the effect it will have on costs, output, safety, etc. This works well with devices.

Since we are concerned with people situations, we must ask ourselves two similar questions concerning our planned method or technique of implementing the scheme:

What is the worst thing that can happen?
What is the best thing that can happen?

Unless these evaluations are consciously conducted you will not be prepared to react to early measurements of your program's success or failure. Not only that, you won't have the absolute evaluation of whether or not you want to take the step at all.

In preparing your speech before the AFL-CIO National Convention, you might decide to make a strong plea for the legal abolishment of all labor unions. Upon reflection, the best thing that could happen would be for your audience to politely ignore what to them would be an outrageous suggestion. The worst (and probable) happening would be to be torn limb from limb right there in the auditorium. Since the result is obvious in advance, you might temper your remarks (if you're bound to say it) to a recommendation that they consider an approach other than the one they are now using. Said approach to be based on the accumulated wisdom present before you. The difference is that instead of being considered a hopeless radical you now become a statesman, and they just might do something.

The situation of the new plant is intended as a case study to permit a closer examination of the situation-prevention concepts discussed above.

The Situation of the New Plant

7he Elf Corporation, a leading supplier of relays to electronic-system manufacturers, located their primary facilities in the New York and Chicago areas due to the highly technical aspects of their work. However, labor and land costs were rising and Elf management decided that it would be profitable to place a manufacturing facility in a more remote, low-cost area. Their plan was to establish a mass-production facility employing from 300 to 500 people who would be involved only in manufacturing. Design and development work would continue to be conducted at the main plants.

As soon as the board made its decision, the company came under siege by the industrial commissions of various states. Site studies were conducted and, after careful deliberation, the company decided to establish its plant in Dalton, Missibama. Dalton had a population of 25,000, was a county seat, had both rail and river transportation, and was only 1 hour by superhighway from the largest city in the region.

The Dalton industrial development board was delighted at the decision. They offered all assistance in establishing the new plant. The state of Missibama allocated various tax and property concessions to make the move easier for Elf. Everyone was happy, except of course the development boards that lost out. Dalton was looking forward to 500 additional jobs and an income increase of 4 million dollars a year.

Charles Barry, operations director of Elf-Chicago, was chosen to install the new plant and serve as its general manager. Barry had been training himself for this opportunity all through his career. He readily agreed when the Elf president said, "Charlie, this time we are going to do it right, all the way. I want you to establish an operation that will be a credit to the corporation and the community. If you need anything from me, speak right up. You are in complete charge of the move. I've arranged that you can take 30 people with you and, as far as I'm concerned, you can have anyone in the corporation you want. Good Luck!"

Barry selected his team.

Personnel was a key spot, considering that he had to take local people who knew very little about the electronics business and turn them into production workers. Because of this, he chose Al Gray from the training department. Al was young, presentable, and energetic. He was very pleased to accept the transfer and promotion.

Frank Schlick, the manufacturing director, had worked for Barry in Chicago. No one in the business knew more than Schlick about setting up assembly operations. Schlick was happy with his new job, because it represented an opportunity rarely presented to men nearing retirement.

Randolph Bergan, also from Chicago, joined the team as

quality control and test manager. Barry felt that his major strength to the team would be his technical competence. Bergan was not particularly pleased about leaving Chicago, but recognized an opportunity when he saw it.

Headquarters supplied a public relations man to the staff to assist Barry through the first year or so. His name was Milo Park, and he had recently joined the company after several years at an advertising agency.

Veteran managers were selected for purchasing, production control, and manufacturing engineering.

When his staff selection was complete, the move was started to Dalton. Through cooperation with Dalton real estate people, all transferred employees were settled comfortably, and the operation began.

After several days of discussion and planning, Barry and his team published their operations plan (Exhibit I). They stuck to it carefully, updating when necessary.

For the first year, until the new plant was built, Elf used warehouse space in the city to establish the first production efforts, train the people, and get established. They were never quite able to reach the output as planned, but Barry felt that this was due to the facilities and that things would be different when they moved into the new plant. The plant was being constructed by a St. Louis firm that specialized in electronic assembly layouts. It would be the most modern in the region. In fact, it would be the most modern in the relay business.

Eight months after moving into the new plant, Charles Barry was called back to headquarters as staff assistant to the manufacturing director. This job was traditionally held open for executives who had failed. It gave them time to find another job, whether they wanted one or not.

Barry could not understand why he had been pulled off the job. True, the plant output had never reached the level anticipated; true, the plant had been unionized almost immediately; and true, it was difficult to get management people to stay in Dalton. He asked the president for specific reasons for his apparent failure but received nothing but generalities. The company was just unhappy with the progress of the operation. The new general manager requested a task force from corporate headquarters and started the rebuilding job. Barry was bewildered.

Perhaps we could help Mr. Barry if we discussed his program.

Q. Mr. Barry, how did you see your job?

A. My immediate purpose was to establish a new plant that would start making a profit at the earliest opportunity. To do this it was necessary to staff it, train people, create an inventory, and begin to manufacture. My long-range purpose was to have the plant continue to function and improve, over the years, until it became the most profitable in the corporation.

Q. What priority did you use in establishing your operation?

A. My first step, of course, was picking my team. Since the plant was to be used primarily for manufacturing, I wanted a strong manufacturing team. I had to do with less experienced men in the service areas. Secondly, I wanted to be sure that our facility would be ready on time and well designed. So we picked a St. Louis company to develop and build the plant. They brought their experienced people in and did the job in record time. Everyone admits that there isn't a better laid-out plant in the corporation. We won a building magazine award for plant design too.

The third step, and it actually was in parallel with the second, was the creation of a basic manufacturing set up, the hiring and training of people, and the actual output. We had to use temporary buildings but it worked out all right. We hired local people as much as we could and used the state employment commission to help us weed them out so we could get

EXHIBIT 1. OPERATIONS PLAN

Activity	Jul 1	Jul 2	Jul 3	Jul 4	Aug 1	Aug 2	Aug 3	Aug 4	Sep 1	Sep 2	Sep 3	Sep 4	Oct 1	Oct 2	Oct 3	Oct 4	Nov 1	Nov 2	Nov 3	Nov 4	Dec 1	Dec 2	Dec 3	Dec 4	Jan 1	Jan 2	Jan 3	Jan 4	Feb 1	Feb 2	Feb 3	Feb 4	Mar 1	Mar 2	Mar 3	Mar 4	Apr 1	Apr 2	Apr 3	Apr 4
Set up office	x																																							
Move key personnel to Dalton	x																																							
Obtain temporary manufacturing space		x	x																																					
Personnel office opens			x																																					
Inventory established			x																																					
Develop manufacturing schedules				x	x																																			
Install equipment							x	x																	x	x														
Personnel training							x			x																														
Production starts								x																																
Ground breaking—new plant										x																														
Construction starts											x																													
Plant layout verification												x	x																											
Board of directors visits											x																													
First product shipment												x	x																											
New equipment approval												x				x	x																							
Management club meetings														x								x								x				x						
Start policy guide book																	x																							
Production scheduling meetings					x	x			x	x			x	x			x	x			x	x			x	x			x	x			x	x					x	x
Start move to new plant																																	x							
Move completed																															x									
Clean up temporary buildings and return																																	x							
Dedication—new plant																																		x						
Personnel training																																	x					x		
First product shipment																																			x					

the most promising ones. These people are not used to manufacturing, you know. They have primarily a farming culture
here. We were forced to bring in some technical people. We
did establish a school for electronics and even made it free,
but we didn't get much attendance.

The last priority was to start meeting the output requirements. I think that these were unrealistic. I always felt that
the headquarter's demands were unrealistic and, in this case,
they proved the point. It isn't possible to have an uninterrupted schedule when you are moving a line several hundred
miles.

Q. How did the local people react to the plant?
A. That was a strange thing. At first they were quite enthu-
    siastic. I went to a couple of chamber of commerce meet-
    ings and sent my industrial relations manager to speak at
    the Rotary. But the people never did seem to accept us. I
    guess it takes a few years. I had a long conversation with
    the bank manager about getting some better loan terms
    for our transferred employees. He didn't seem to think
    that much could be done, and it wasn't. However, there
    has been a good social acceptance in the community;
    some of our men are on the board of the country club
    and are quite at home.
Q. I hope you won't mind my asking. If you had it all to do
    over again, would you do anything differently?
A. I don't think so. I gave this thing a lot of thought before,
    during, and after going down there. I felt then, and I feel
    now, that my actions were in the interest of the corpora-
    tion. It is a real mystery to me that they feel I failed. For
    my own peace of mind, I am going to charge the whole
    thing off to office politics and try again. If you'll excuse
    me I must get to a meeting.

At this point, it would be interesting to evaluate the brief
questioning of Mr. Barry against the three considerations of

Situation Prevention to see if it might give us an insight into his failure. He doesn't feel he failed, but his employers do. Since keeping the boss satisfied with your performance is part of Situation Management, we must conclude that he did indeed fail, even if the reason is not clear.

1. *What are the short- and long-range purposes of this action?*

Barry listed his purpose as establishing a plant to make a profit, staff it, and eventually have it be the most profitable in the corporation. This is a slightly condensed quote, but I think that was the intent of his statement.

His president stated the purpose as "Charlie, this time we are going to do it right, all the way. I want you to establish an operation that will be a credit to the corporation and the community."

Charlie didn't include anything in his purpose about *doing it right* and apparently didn't try to find out what that meant. He interpreted "credit to the corporation" as being profit oriented but did not consider "credit to the community."

Right or wrong, Charlie and his boss started out with different opinions concerning how to measure the total success of the project. Barry would have to be awful lucky to come out with the proper ending, and he was too good at his job to be lucky. He spent his effort on the purpose he had chosen— even if he had achieved it, his president might have thought him a failure. Let's ask the president what he felt the purpose was. (Apparently he could benefit from a little Situation Prevention study too.)

"I wanted to set up this plant as a showplace. It seemed to me that we could present an example of how complex electronic devices could be made in a rural area, and we would be able to eventually move our entire operations to the South. If we kept the plants small enough, we would be able to have old fashioned employee participation, avoid unions, and produce at a constant rate. All we would need up here in the high-rent district would be our development laboratory. With the right success we might even be able to move that. I would have settled for a money-losing operation for a year or two if we could have gotten off to a good start."

Entirely different purposes, entirely different goals—yet each felt he understood the other. Let's consider the second question of Situation Prevention.

2. *Have I prepared the way for the successful completion of this action by establishing positive communications and coordination with those who will be affected by it?*

Charlie concentrated on the manufacturing operation, and his staff selection shows that. The president wanted community relations first.

Why did the people reject the new plant? Why did the union have such an easy organizing job? Why didn't the bank president bend a little and provide the loans that were well within his authority?

All for the same reason—the Elf management ignored the town. They didn't become involved in community affairs as individuals. They sent the second team to the Rotary meeting; and most concrete of all, they brought an entire crew in from St. Louis to build the factory. Certainly an enlightened management would have insisted that the contractor use local labor for the majority of the job. It is all right to get an architect from another town. It is even permissible to have the contractor be experienced; but manual labor, plumbing, masonry, and carpentry can certainly be contracted in the local area. At least an effort can be made. Who can blame the people of Dalton for *having their pride hurt.* They retaliated by ignoring the new plant, thus the low attendance at the electronics school, the susceptibility to union organization.

Barry considered the who of his situation as being those people directly concerned with the day-to-day operation of the plant. He did not bother to try to know or understand the "thought leaders" of Dalton and quickly categorized their culture as farming. It is amazing what preconception can do for a man.

If he had been interested in involving the town in his purpose, he would probably have established an unofficial board of the local leaders to advise him on the proper way to approach the community. It would not be necessary to accept their advice, and they would know that, but at least they would have been considered.

Since there was no cooperative effort discernible, the people naturally felt that the company had little interest in their welfare. The union representatives were smarter; so they offered to assure that such interest was taken.

Thus nothing came out like it was supposed to.

Now how about the third question of Situation Prevention?

3. *Is the implementation method I have chosen the result of a thoughtful situation analysis, including "best" and "worst" case anticipated results, or am I following normal practices?*

Under Charlie Barry's plan the best thing that could happen to him was to make a profit on schedule. This is what could have been expected of him in his opinion; therefore, there was little chance of being a hero by excelling. The worst case probably didn't enter his mind, but it is what happened. He chose a course that led him to be measured on one criterion only. As we know now, he was ignoring the other factors that the president was going to use to measure his success.

The three most important men on Barry's staff were the manufacturing manager, public relations, and industrial relations. Yet he chose proved, competent people in the first category only. He could have had anyone he wanted, but he promoted people—new people.

His implementation plan consisted entirely of a scheduled acquiring of inventory, people, and facilities. It did not take into consideration the effect on the community or the long-range goals of the corporation. He assumed that the corporate goals were unrealistic without finding out their intent.

Charlie Barry will go to his grave convinced that he was "had," and he may be correct in some of his feelings. But it was his responsibility to find out specifically, and in writing, what he was expected to accomplish. He didn't.

If you happen to be acquainted with a large corporation you may find that it has several bright, experienced "staff assistants" who used to be executives and are now hunting for other "challenges." Some of them may have followed Charlie's path to this spot. Some of them may have gotten there through the medium of saying, and implementing, one of these statements:

1. "Don't give me any help. We'll straighten the situation out if corporate will leave us alone."

2. "I know the operation has been losing money for 2 years, but we are going to increase efficiency this year and will turn a profit."

3. "The way to turn this operation around is to cut out all the luxuries so we're eliminating inspection, drawing control, and training."

4. "My people are too busy, and our travel budget is too skimpy, to participate in conferences and meetings."

5. "The customers don't understand."

It might be said that Charlie was dead when he took this assignment. He did not understand what the board wanted, and they didn't understand what he wanted. The fault must be equally shared, but since the organized world is constructed like it is the blame will fall only on one head. Anyone could predict whose head was sacrificed.

It will do no good to pursue the thought that a deeper investigation of management intent must be conducted because it is not possible to go deep enough to unearth every possible desire. Even if you do this, the desires may change due to forces you could not foresee. Therefore, there are only two ways out:

1. Have an ironclad contract that spells out the objective specifically and the terms by which success or failure will be measured. (You have a very fat chance of getting this.)

2. Require constant involvement by those who will be judging.

If Charlie had had periodic meetings with top management to discuss his progress, his future planning, and the problems that existed, he would have become aware very soon that the board was interested in using this operation as a prototype for future expansion and vitally interested in community relationships.

If he didn't know how to handle that, and it is permissible for a general manager to have a void or two in his competence, he could have asked for, and received, guidance and assistance.

In a nutshell, he got so wrapped up on the day-to-day jobs that he forgot to get other people involved. When the inevitable judgment day arrived he had no sympathetic voice speaking for him at the head table. It's as simple as that.

Consider the success record posted by those whom you have known who accepted a difficult job only after insisting that they be left completely alone to work it out as they pleased. Even if the job came off right they always suffered anyway. Ever hear of Sir Walter Raleigh?

The Situation of the Status Report

> "Men are disturbed not by things, but by the view which they take of things" EPICTETUS

Problems exist and will continue to do so regardless of your personal wishes or drives. Their relative seriousness has no bearing on their existence. Problems exist because they are and because each human has a problem bucket that aches to be filled. Where there are no problems, people will create some. Witness the Garden of Eden; observe ancient Carthage; remember Edward Kent.

Who was Edward Kent? I don't know. His name was listed only to permit you to observe yourself creating a problem for you. "Why don't I know about Edward Kent when I know about Eden and Carthage? Should I look it up? How can I have reached this age and never heard of anyone obviously that famous?"

We seek problems. They rarely seek us. It is our duty as Situation Managers to organize ourselves for the controlling of the *daily problem list* that is anxiously scanned by those whose activities and attitudes are important to us. Controlling, or at least understanding, this list is the Situation Manager's forte.

The first consideration is: *How do we tell a problem?*

Those new to the Situation Management business may conceive that a problem is a problem and that to report it is quite easy, since you only list the facts so that others may then know what has happened and act wisely to overcome it. Unfortunately, the problem itself has little to do with how people will react. They react independently of the situation itself and are concerned only with making sure that their personal needs are achieved. This is true regardless of the dedication and compassion residing within their soul. The missionary is going to convert the cannibal even if it means being digested; the professional ball player is going to score even if it means causing his opponent to be fired thus taking the bread from the mouths of children; the mother will save her children if it means *wiping out* half the town.

If we are to practice telling a problem, we must consider it through the mind of the person we want to impress, motivate, or mollify. Consider the sinking of the *Titanic*. How would it look as seen through the eyes of:

A naturalist:

SHIP ATTACKS ICEBERG

In the early hours of today, the world's largest ship, coldly and without warning, viciously attacked iceberg 23 who was floating along minding her own business. Twenty-three suffered a large gash in her port side but courageously righted herself, shook off the ship, and proceeded bravely on her way. A protest has been filed with the British Ministry.

A Maritime labor leader:

1,800 JOBS LOST

Through the carelessness of the British Ministry, the *Titanic* has been permitted to ram an iceberg and sink. As a result, the maritime union has lost 1,800 berths for their members.

This is obviously a plot to ruin the union and make us beg for jobs. A protest has been filed with the British Ministry.

A merchant:

WOOLENS RUINED

Our spring showing will be delayed because the material being shipped from the British mills has been permitted to become waterlogged, due to the sinking of the *Titanic*. As a result of this plot to drive the woolen prices higher, we are considering purchasing our next order from New Zealand. A protest has been filed with the British Ministry.

The only purpose of reporting a problem is to create a desire for action on the part of those to whom you are reporting it. You must be able to hit upon the right group of words if you are to achieve your purpose. You want something done and you want it done now! (Sometimes it is not necessary to mention the real problem.)

How would you report these situations in order to get action?

1. The boiler in your plant is well past retirement age. However, capital expenditures for replacement have been refused. Your engineer feels that it is going to go in the next few days. If so, it will shut you down for several weeks due to the damage the failure will create. However, if you can obtain the money you can put in a new one over the weekend.

2. A department store is continually dunning you to pay a bill that you do not owe. When contacted by telephone, they apologize for their computer and assure you that everything will be all right next month. When next month rolls around, the computer threatens you with a visit from the sheriff.

3. Your daughter has decided to become a polo player.

When you report a problem, you want someone to do something which will result in eliminating its existence—for you. Therefore, you must, although sticking to facts, tell the problem in the proper manner. For instance:

Problem No. 1

Q. Who needs to be influenced?

A. Top management.

Q. What concerns them most?

A. Loss of profit or presence of public sensation.

Q. What do I want?

A. A new boiler.

Combine the two and you have the following report.

> TO: Top Management
> FROM: Plant No. 6
>
> We request approval of the attached emergency procedure. In the event of a predicted boiler explosion, we have arranged for civil defense personnel to assist with the injured. Production operations will be moved to the warehouse. It is felt that only 3 weeks of output will be lost and that we will be able to produce 45 percent of our regular commitment during that time period. We should be back on schedule 6 months after the explosion.

Problem No. 2

Q. Who needs to be influenced?

A. The department store's credit department.

Q. What concerns them most?

A. People paying their bills on time and the store's reputation.

Q. What do I want?

A. Them to state my bill correctly and quit bothering me.

Combine the two and you have the following report:

> TO: Credit Department
> FROM: Citizens for Accurate Billing
>
> We have selected your store as an example of computerized billing and are considering presenting you with our award of excellence. We plan to take a poll of your customers in the next few weeks, and if we find no cases of duplicate

or erroneous billing, you will be notified that you have won the award.

(Nothing says you can't set up a one-man committee.)

Problem No. 3

Q. Who needs to be influenced?

A. Your daughter.

Q. What concerns her most?

A. Her personal beauty, and her urge for adventure.

Combine the two and you have the following report:

> TO: Daughter
> FROM: Father
>
> Congratulations on deciding to take up polo instead of swimming. It is a fine sport. Not only is riding a horse excellent exercise but it is broadening. Excuse my little joke. Love, Dad.

Now you may note that the subject has been slightly changed in each example. Therein lies the secret of proper problem reporting if you wish to excell as a Situation Manager. Problems are all in the way you look at them. Problem reporting is to get other people to look at problems the same way you do.

Let's see how one man reported his problems:

"Let's look at the facts, old boy," said George Elmhurst to himself. "Just list the facts as they are, no shilly-shallying, no mish-mash. Just give the bare basics and let the chips fall where they may."

> TO: President, Friendly Corporation
> FROM: George Elmhurst, General Manager, Components Division
> SUBJECT: Quarterly Status Report
>
> The overall situation at components is very poor. We are 23 percent under budget in production output. Customers have returned 9 percent of the products shipped during the quarter due to poor quality. Sales orders are dropping every

day, and it looks as if we will wind up under our sales budget by at least 30 percent. The union is very unhappy about projected layoffs; and their leaders are talking about a strike to guarantee job security; also, we need a capital appropriation of $123,540 to replace the plating facility.

I would appreciate some assistance from corporate staff.

Very truly yours,
George

"Oh boy," thought George, "I can see the old man going through the roof now. He won't even give me a chance to explain when he reads this letter. Most of it isn't my fault, or the fault of anyone here in the component division. Perhaps I'd better give this a good think."

Since George has no choice but to follow our procedure, let us now proceed to an analysis of this situation according to the questions of Situation Prevention. We shall assume that George has vuluntarily decided to do this himself. His motivation may be classed as one of sheer desperation.

1. What are the short- and long-range purposes of this action?

Short-range—to fulfill the requirement of telling headquarters what is going on each quarter.

Long-range—to get some help in this impossible situation I have on my hands. Sales is corporate. The union is making its own rules, and the customers are getting the wrong idea of what our products are supposed to do for them.

2. Have I prepared the way for the successful completion of this action by establishing communications and coordination with those who will be affected? Holy mackerel! I have never asked for headquarter's help up to now. In fact, I have ignored it. But really, they are part of the problem. Perhaps I should request a total evaluation, but that might cause me problems too. The answer must be that so far I have not prepared the way. I'd better start preparing it. That means that I will have to explain my problems in such a way as to make them feel compassionate toward this division.

3. Is the implementation method I have chosen the result of a

thoughtful situation analysis, including "best" and "worst" case anticipated results or am I following normal practices? I have not really thought about the thing. I have merely followed the reports of my staff. There are probably better ways of doing things. If I send in the report as it was written, I'll be fired. If I surpress it, I'll be fired too. At this point, I think I'd better take a look at this total situation and examine the problems one at a time.

While Mr. Elmhurst is wrestling with his next move, let's review the history of his experience at the component division of the Friendly Corporation.

George joined Friendly 3 years ago. He had been a plant general manager prior to that time and was looking for greater things in his career. At Friendly he became assistant to the executive vice-president for a year in order to learn the corporation and at the same time provide some of his expertise to the component operation. Components was a growing operation, but it was losing money. Friendly had decided to enter the field starting from scratch and had anticipated that it would take them 6 years to start receiving a return on their investment. At the end of 6 years the division was still losing money and returning a minus 9 percent on sales. The tax-loss days were behind them and something had to be done. The board debated the alternatives of getting out of the business altogether or trying one more time. Since the potential looked so favorable, they decided that they would purchase another company in the field, Flower, and merge it with their own components division. Their real target was the management of Flower and in particular, the boy wonder of the components field, Harvey Harrison. Harvey had brought Flower from nothing to something in only 4 years.

The deal was consummated. The units were merged and the struggle started anew. The business projection that Harvey brought forth for the next 2 years indicated that the combined component operation would soon be pushing the big boys out of the field and promised a break, even by the end of the first year, and an 8 percent return, at the end of the second. Everyone was pleased except George Elmhurst who thought the plan overly ambitious. George recognized that he had anticipated obtaining responsibility for those divisions, and so quieted his fears by reminding himself that he was just jealous.

Harvey operated. He centralized the manufacturing operations. He moved sales to corporate, in order to more efficiently handle the broadened line; and he cut the overhead. (George noted that most of the cuts were among the Friendly personnel and that the Flower people were pretty much in control of the operation.)

But it just wouldn't move.

At the end of the first year Harvey threw up his hands ("to collect a large stock offer from another company," thought George) and resigned. George was thrust into the gap as division general manager and instructed to pull the job out of the hole. He applied all his skill; worked increasingly hard hours; cultivated and developed his team; and, as a result, found himself facing the last quarter of the year predicting not an 8 percent return but a minus 15 percent loss.

It is at this point that we join George preparing his quarterly report.

"I think I know all the problems," mused George, "but I'm not getting very far with the solution. Perhaps I should try to spell the thing out one line at a time by utilizing the Situation Management procedure."

AWARENESS

1. *What seems to be the situation?*

This division is losing money. Hard work and desire have not changed it. I am faced with reporting personal failure to headquarters; yet, in my heart, I feel that we have done everything that could be done under the present plan.

2. *How did I find out that the situation existed?*

The cost figures are accurate. I know that, because we just revised the accounting procedure 3 months ago. That's when I discovered that we were being too kind to ourselves in the inventory and capital areas. Of course the place has been a money loser all along.

3. *What is the potential effect of this matter?*

For me it could mean the end of a fine relationship. For the division—disaster. For the corporation—a loss of face and capital.

4. *How serious is it?*

Very serious. I think this may be the end of the road.

5. *How much time do I have to extricate myself?*

About 1 week. That is when the report is due at headquarters.

EVALUATION

1. *What evidence leads me to believe the situation exists?*

Performance data. Reports of sales, schedule, product quality, and costs.

2. *What is the specific source of this evidence?*

It comes from the comptroller's office, quality control, and the sales department.

3. *Do I know this evidence is factual?*

I have checked it out in sufficient detail to know that it is an accurate portrayal of our situation.

4. *Could I list the steps that created the situation?*

Yes, but I don't think anyone would like it. We tried to be born whole, producing a complete line. We didn't have the established customers and have had to sell on price, while promising product performance in excess of our competitors. To achieve this, we attempted to motivate our people to perform impossible tasks and bought the skills to do so. We have tried to purchase success.

5. *Whose mind must I change to resolve the problem?*
The president and the board.

6. *What do those minds think now?*
They think that the only thing missing in this operation is hard work and time. They also think the time has run out and it may need some harder workers.

7. *How will I know when the situation has been successfully resolved?*
When the division starts returning a profit and the board thinks I am the greatest thing since "hot pants."

ACTION
1. *Join the key individuals and the key issues.*
The board feels that the failure of this division to be successful is the result of poor management on my part.

2. *Why do they believe this?*
Because the success plan was created by a man with a long history of achievement, and in addition the board created the operating policy.

3. *What would it require to separate them from this opinion?*
They would have to be shown factually that the approach we are trying cannot possibly succeed and to be offered a foolproof plan that will sell components.

4. *What is the best method to use in this separation?*
We need to review the whole operation, determine a different strategy, and realign ourselves to meet it.

5. *How do I implement the method?*
I would have to obtain the board's attention long enough to make the presentation without being fired, and then get them to participate long enough to become part of the solu-

tion. Really, I think all we need to do is cut our calalog down to where we are peddling the things that are selling anyway and drop the loss items.

6. *Once it is over what steps do I take to assure that it will never happen again?*

I promise that I will never take over an operation unless I have been able to create the performance plan myself.

At this point, our hero took pen in hand once more and addressed his report to the president of Friendly.

TO: President, Friendly Corporation
FROM: George Elmhurst, General Manager, Components Division
SUBJECT: Quarterly Status Report

1. You know from the weekly reports that we are falling behind on sales and output. In addition, our warranty costs are 9 percent of sales. Inventory is over the budget 18 percent, and the union is threatening to strike.

2. I have verified all of these items. In my opinion, they will become a more serious exposure during the next quarter unless we take some drastic action.

3. These problems are only symptoms of the deeper situation involving us. Our real problems are:

a. Our product line is too wide. I am attaching a list of money losers that I recommend we cut out tomorrow. I know that sales will say they must have a full line in order to obtain orders, but we are just going to have to decide that this is no longer true.

b. We have patterned our specifications and our processes after our competitors' products.

c. We must develop some proprietary products.

d. Our quality problems will go away when we start delivering what we know we have, but I feel we must investigate the customer's requirements in more detail and test to the same methods they use.

e. We must tell the union that if they will not go along with us on cutting back the work force in order to meet these commitments, we will close the plant, and mean it.

4. If we are not willing to do these things, I recommend going out of the components business.

5. A change of management will not alter the facts now before us. "New blood" will only create new promises until they begin to comprehend the situation it has taken me 9 months to understand.

6. If you are agreeable to these moves, I request that you provide me with a corporate staff task team consisting of industrial engineers, reliability and quality control people, marketing survey personnel, and an inventory specialist. I will need them for 2 months. If I am correct, we will break even in 6 months and turn our first profit, a modest 1 percent, in 8 months.

7. If you do not feel that you can accept these action recommendations, I would appreciate the opportunity to transfer to another position within the corporation. If that is not possible, then I shall resign at your request.

> Respectfully,
> George Elmhurst

"Now," thought George, "that ought to spell it out clearly enough. After reading it over, I think I'll remove the 'Respectfully'; even the old man would think that was laying it on a little thick. Let's see how this solution would work out."

1. *What is the short- and long-range purpose of this action?*
Short-range is to get myself some time to do the things that I now know must be done. Long-range is to actually get this operation making money.

2. *Have I prepared the way for the successful completion of this action by establishing communications and coordination with those who will be affected?*
I've started it. There is no use going to the union, or the staff people until I've been told by the president whether or not he will accept my ideas. However, in order to make sure that at least this much of the communication is effected, I think I will take it to him instead of mailing it. He doesn't

like the division managers to leave the operations. Seeing me there will add emphasis to the seriousness of the matter

3. *Is the implementation method I have chosen the result of a thoughtful situation analysis, including "best" and "worst" case anticipated results, or am I following normal practices?*

I think I have done a proper analysis on this one. It would be possible to "phony" the thing along for another quarter or two until I found myself another job, but this has to be the best way—face up to the problem and fight it.

The best thing that can happen is that they go along with me and we are successful. The worst thing is that I get fired. No, wait a minute, the really worst thing is that I get fired and someone else comes in, operates to the old plan, and makes money. Can that happen? No, I don't believe it can.

George took his plan to headquarters. To his surprise the president listened carefully, interrogated incisively, and then —agreed. George went back to work and 8 months later returned a profit of 1.8 percent.

He often wondered what made this all come about. There are several possible solutions. Perhaps the president was waiting all this time for someone to create his own plan. Perhaps George could only make something work that he invented. Perhaps his plan was the only way. I will let the reader decide. The important aspect is that George evaluated his situation properly, took action steps, knew where he was going, and went there.

Beware the "I's" of Situation Management

"And every star and every whirling plant,
And every constellation in the sky,
Revolves around the center of the universe:
That lovely thing called I."

—OSCAR HAMMERSTEIN

*T*he problem most of us face when starting to use Situa
tion Management is that we forget that not only are we
ourselves part of the situation, but more likely we have
contributed a great deal to its existence. It takes at least
two for a conflict.

In order to overcome this natural tendency, we must
look very honestly at each situation to assess our personal
contribution to its solution.

If you remember back in "The Situation of the Boss
versus Peace and Quiet," Harry, our hero, helped cause
the situation to occur by forgetting to keep in touch with
his counterparts. Tom Johnson in "The Situation of the

Unwanted Improvement" helped cause his problem by taking his eye off the doughnut while detailing the dimensions of the hole in infinite detail. It can happen to anyone.

Some years ago I was quality manager of a missile program. One of my areas of responsibilities was the inspection and test of the missiles before they were sent to the test range for firing. To conduct these tests, as well as other ones, I had a very large department, the latest in special and complex equipment, competent people, and the absolute support and encouragement of the company's management.

When the birds would arrive at the test range, they would be checked out by the customer's people, as well as engineers from our own company. Each report the range filed listed some errors. They would consistently find six or seven things wrong with the missile. These ranged all the way from a plant scratch to an uncaged gyro.

But considering the complexity of the system, it must have had at least 50,000 parts, I wasn't too concerned. We seemed to be getting better each time, and I knew for sure that our faults were a lot less numerous than those of other programs. However, the customer kept getting upset and soon my own management was snapping at me.

I kept explaining the laws of probability, showing improvement curves, and, in general, trying to get them to understand that they couldn't expect things to get much better as long as mere people were involved.

But the pressure continued and signs began to appear that perhaps I should worry about Law No. 1. And in spite of myself, I sat down to give the thing a good think. "Why were these people being so unreasonable?"

Obviously they had not had the experience in the things of quality that I had. Just as obviously, they were not going to let me stay around long enough to teach them this experience. There had to be a way out.

Up to this time, I had assumed that I was not part of the

problem, or that if I were, it was only because I had failed to educate my leaders properly. Then it occurred to me that I was very happy with six or seven defects per bird and that perhaps my people recognized this. They were apparently meeting my standard. They also weren't upset.

Therefore, I called all the supervisors together and told them that from now on our standard was no defects. *Zero Defects* is what I wrote on the board. They argued for a few moments, shrugged, and went back to work. Two deliveries later, the people at the test range could find nothing wrong with the missile and told us so. After that, Zero Defects became routine. Once in a while something would slip through. Everyone would raise Cain, and we would get back to doing the job right.

Now it is apparent that what had happened was that we had proved that a dedicated crew of competent people with the proper equipment can find all the defects or problems in a system. However, that is very expensive. Thus, working on the basis that the problem is the standards of management (the product looks like the manager), and not the work standards of the people, I constructed the concept of Zero Defects for the purpose of preventing defects.

The concept goes like this:

"The products of industry are not good enough, customer complaints are rising, and there is too much waste. Those products that work trouble-free do so because of an investment in test, inspection, and service that is out of proportion. Many companies spend 10, 15, and even 20 percent of their sales dollar on scrap, rework, warranty, service, test, and inspection. The errors that produce this waste are caused directly by the personnel of the plant, both employees and management.

"To eliminate this waste, to improve the operation, to become more efficient, we must concentrate on preventing the defects and errors that plague us. The defect that is prevented doesn't need repair, examination, or explanation.

"The first step is to examine and adopt the attitude of defect prevention. This attitude is called, symbolically: *Zero Defects.*

"Zero Defects is a standard for management, a standard that management can convey to the employees to help them to decide to 'Do the job right the first time.'

"People are conditioned to believe that error is inevitable. We not only accept error, we anticipate it. Whether we are designing circuits, planning a project, soldering joints, typing letters, completing an account ledger, or assembling components, it does not bother us to make a few errors—and management plans for these errors to occur. We feel that human beings have a 'built in' error factor.

"However, we do not naintain the same standard when it comes to our personal life. If we did, we would resign ourselves to being shortchanged now and then as we cash our pay checks. We would expect hospital nurses to drop a certain percent of all newborn babies. We would expect to go home to the wrong house by mistake periodically. As individuals we do not tolerate these things. Thus we have a double standard—one for ourselves, one for the company.

"The reason for this is the family creates a higher performance standard for us than the company does.

"In short, we must determine if we as management have made our desires clear to those who look to us for guidance and direction. We must provide an understandable, constant standard for quality performance.

"Consider the three basic areas of performance in any organization: cost, schedule, and quality.

"All of these are vital for success. Each requires the establishment of a performance standard that cannot be misunderstood.

"Take cost. Everyone understands what two dollars and thirty four cents looks like. There may be some argument about what to do with money, but everyone understands its substance. A budget is set and the standard is to make the job and the funds come out together.

"Schedule also has an understandable common base: time. We all use the same standard calendars and clocks. Delivery and completion dates are specified in contracts and requirements. We either meet the dates or we do not.

"Now what is the existing standard for quality?

"Most people talk about an AQL—an acceptable quality level. An AQL really means a commitment before we start the job to produce imperfect material. Let me repeat, an acceptable quality level is a commitment before we start the job that we will produce imperfect material. An AQL, therefore, is not a management standard. It is a determination of the status quo. Instead of the managers' setting the standard, the operation sets the standard.

"Consider the AQL you would establish on the product you buy. Would you accept an automobile that you knew in advance was 15 percent defective? 5 percent? 1 percent? ½ of 1 percent? How about the nurses that care for newborn babies? Would an AQL of 3 percent on mishandling be too rigid?

"The Zero Defects concept is based on the fact that mistakes are caused by two things: lack of knowledge and lack of attention.

"Lack of knowledge can be measured and attacked by tried and true means. But lack of attention is a state of mind. It is an attitude problem that must be changed by the person himself. When presented with the challenge to do this, and the encouragement to attempt it, the individual will respond enthusiastically. Remember—Zero Defects is not a motivation method, it is a performance standard. And it is not just for production people, it is for everyone. Some of the biggest gains occur in the nonproduction areas.

"The Zero Defects program must be personally directed by top management.

"People receive their standards from their leaders. They

perform to the requirements given to them. They must be told that your personal standard is—Zero Defects.

"To gain the benefits of Zero Defects, you must decide to make a personal commitment to have improvement in your operation. You must want it.

"The first step is: Make the attitude of Zero Defects your personal standard."

Now that seemed clear to me. However, I found people thinking that Zero Defects was a worker motivation program and blaming all the problems on the workers. For years I have made speeches and written articles saying that it wasn't motivation, saying that the management is the bad guy, and trying to have the professionals recognize that we are dealing with a new management philosophy, not a propaganda program. To no avail.

The fact that Zero Defects has succeeded so well over the years is due to the intelligence of the workers who took it for what it is supposed to be. How did I fail in explaining it? I assumed that everyone had gone through the same emotional experience I did. The thinking will be corrected some day, but it won't be because I did the job right the first time.

When you analyze a problem through the use of the Situation Analysis guide, always use the Situation Prevention guide as a check on yourself to make sure that in your eagerness to express your brilliant solution, you have not overlooked something. What you feel is not always apparent to others.

Getting Paid
for Doing Something
Doesn't Make You a Pro

*A*nother of the problems of getting people to take Situation Management seriously is, of course, that they feel they don't need it. After all, they are employed in a significant position; are adequately pampered by their company, family, and staff; and can point with pride to their successful fight to attain their present position. They can look back to the tough days and identify for you the guys who didn't make it. They may even recount modestly some of the things they did to make life a little happier for those unfortunates.

But if you note the tone of the conversation and the impact of their concern, you may be surprised to realize that it is primarily past-oriented.

The programs and disciplines they are now conducting are modifications of previous triumphs. More and more personal action is required to make them come true each time. The executive finds himself working harder than ever before, surely only one of the simple badges of success. He would be glad to discuss Situation Management with you, but he has difficulty thinking he needs it. Every sensible man already knows these things. He feels you should discuss it with the less experienced members of his organization. If they were doing their work better, he would have time for such things.

He thinks he is a pro.

But what are the characteristics of a professional?

The pro wins anyhow. He is in control of his skills. He commands his own time. He gets the required results with a minimum of effort. While he may receive setbacks now and then, he views these as merely a source of reeducation.

He is relaxed, confident, and poised. He knows everything that is going on around him, and he strikes (to coin a phrase) when the iron is hot—and only then. He knows the precise moment to move. There is no wasted motion.

It is the presence of wasted motion that identifies the non-pro. Since he is not in control, he must participate in everything to make sure he isn't left out. If you throw enough balls at the hoop, you are going to sink one now and then. Working long hours and being involved with a lot of things on this basis is absolute identification of the nonpro.

Take the matter of setting objectives. There are really only two types: personal and business. Ask the nonpro about his personal objectives and he will immediately detail something unmeasurable and probably pious.

"I want to be a good husband and father."

"I'd like to do my part in improving the world."

The pro is specific.

"I want to provide my children with the education they need and give them $50,000 each for a financial start in life."

"I will head up the Salvation Army fund-raising drive and collect 1 million dollars for them."

It is in the matter of company or department objectives that the difference between the two approaches becomes blatantly apparent. The pro never sets an objective that doesn't contain a measurement. The nonpro wouldn't dream of including one.

"Improve customer relations," "reduce operating costs," "upgrade our quality," "increase efficiency"—these are all nonpro objectives.

"Reduce customer complaints by 23 percent in 12 months," "reduce operating costs by 4.5 percent of sales while maintaining present output," "reduce defects per unit from 6 to 0.5 in the first quarter," "raise productivity from 86 percent to 94 percent by July 1"—these are pro goals. People can understand them.

Which type are you?

Situations to Practice Preventing By

<u>S</u>ituation No. 1 You have been given the job of establishing standard operating procedures in the 57 regional offices of your company. You have no staff other than a secretary you share with another man. You decide to write the operating procedures, issue them, and then conduct a series of seminars so that all the area office managers can learn how to comply with the procedures.

Use the Situation Prevention guide to see how you are going to make out.

<u>Situation No. 2</u> You have been appointed to the Board of Regents of your Alma Mater, a private school. The Student Committee for Academic Freedom has just submitted a petition to the board requesting the right to participate in the annual performance review of faculty members. The faculty is up in arms at this request. The

board has asked you to talk with the representatives of each group and develop a solution. You listen to both stories, decide that the students have a case, and recommend that they be permitted to participate.

Use the Situation Prevention guide to see how you are going to make out.

<u>Situation No. 3</u> You receive a letter from the Internal Revenue Service telling you that they have decided to audit your tax form. The only item you can think of that they might question is your practice of deducting one room in the house as an office. Therefore, you invite the agent to do the auditing at your house so you can seat him at your desk and let him use your adding machine.

Use the Situation Prevention guide to see how you are going to make out.

<u>Situation No. 4</u> Business is somewhat less than sensational. It is apparent that severe cutbacks will have to be made. You are assigned the task. After reviewing the budget situation, you recommend a 15 percent cut across the board. Every department is told to cut 15 percent immediately. Your cost reduction goal is met. Was this a good decision?

Situations 1 and 4 are discussed in detail on the following pages. Numbers 2 and 3 are up to you.

Test Situation No. 1

1. *What is the short- and long-range purpose of this action?*

Short-range is to establish a set of operating procedures that will fit all of the offices and get the office managers to start using them. Long-range is to have the procedures proved to be very successful in terms of cost savings and efficiency, so that I can get recognition and be promoted to a good job.

2. *Have I prepared the way for the successful completion of this action by establishing communications and coordination with those who will be affected?*

I have done half of it. That is, my boss knows about it because he gave me the assignment. When I start having the seminars on the procedures, the office managers will know about it. However, they won't have anything to say about the content of the procedures or the way they are to be implemented. They will come in cold—that might not be too good.

3. *Is the implementation method I have chosen the result of a thoughtful situation analysis, including "best" and "worst"-case anticipated results, or am I following normal practices?*

Guilty. I have just picked out a traditional method, actually like the type used by an army. The best thing that would happen would be that they would accept and use the procedures I developed. The worst thing would be that the procedures wouldn't be adequate and would cause more problems than we now have. Another worst could be that they would feel left out and not participate at all. (Laws 2, 4, and 6.)

4. *How am I going to make out?*

Not very well. I better do a Situation Analysis on this.

AWARENESS

1. *What seems to be the situation?*

I am about to write up a bunch of procedures to be used by all our office managers. I'm not sure the procedures will be adequate or that they would use them anyway.

2. *How did I find out that the situation exists?*

I didn't really. However, I used to be an office manager and I don't feel I would have liked being handled in the way I was going to do it.

3. *What is the potential effect of this matter?*

If I don't get the cooperation of the office managers, then the whole bit is dead, including me.

4. *How serious is it?*
Critical.

5. *How much time do I have to extricate myself?*

A lot of time. I didn't start anything yet, and so there is nothing to undo. I have time to get smart, perhaps 6 or 7 months.

EVALUATION

1. *What evidence leads me to believe that the situation exists?*

My own personal experience, plus Laws of Situation Management 2, 4, and 6.

2. *What is the specific source of this evidence?*

When I was an office manager, I resented receiving any direction from headquarters. Also, it is apparent that since none of the 57 managers involved are demanding that all offices operate alike, they haven't thought much about it. This program is not exactly the people's choice.

3. *Do I know that the evidence is factual?*

I think I'm going to have to take a trip around the company to make sure. However, my own past experience is certainly factual, and I have seen enough to believe that the laws are true.

4. *Could I list the steps that created the situation?*

I guess it started when I just pulled a traditional solution out of my pocket without thinking about the particular situation we have here.

5. *Whose mind must I change to resolve the problem?*

Mine is already changed. That leaves the 57 office managers.

6. *What does that mind think now?*

I'm going to have to go see for sure, but it seems to me they think that things are probably all right now and that they don't need to have a new set of procedures for the purpose of coordinating something that they do not feel is a problem.

7. *How will I know when the situation is resolved?*

When all the necessary procedures and disciplines have been developed and are operated by happy managers.

ACTION

1. *Join the key individuals and the key issues.*

Our office managers don't see a need for unified procedures, but my boss does. I have to figure a way of having the procedures developed and implemented.

2. *Why do they believe this?*

The office managers only see their own operations. They really think the others don't have any effect on them. My boss sees lots of them. He knows differently.

3. *What would it require to separate them from this belief?*

Getting the office managers to talk with each other about their problems.

4. *What is the best method to use in this separation?*

Bringing some of them together, so that they can learn their problems are similar, and generating in them the desire to help each other.

5. *How do I implement the method?*

If I picked several of the biggest offices and brought their men together for a meeting, and handled it right, they might get the idea of inviting the rest to join in a common effort. I should prepare a presentation showing them the results, in dollars, of not having common procedures and practices.

6. *Once it is over, what steps do I take to assure that it will never happen again?*

Keep the communications going by making sure that the organization becomes formalized.

After thinking this out, our hero did indeed invite several of the key office managers to get together. His presentation showed them the inefficiency involved. It also showed them that he didn't know how to resolve it. They appointed some study teams, asked the other managers to join them for an organizational meeting, and identified the necessary procedures. Using their headquarters' contact as a coordinator (and banner bearer), they attacked the problem of developing and implementing the procedures. Since the offices themselves were involved, the new procedures were accepted easily.

Obviously this took some time and a great deal of Situation Management. But it is doubtful if it could be done by any other manner. It is well known that the mere making and issuing of procedures from headquarters has little to do with their use. This way everyone participated. Everyone got some credit, and the procedures themselves probably were better than one man could have developed anyway.

Test Situation No. 4

1. *What is the short- and long-range purpose of this action?*

Short-range is to reduce our expenditures immediately so the company will not suffer a loss. Long-range is to permit us to ride out this recession period and come back strong when things improve.

2. *Have I prepared the way for the successful completion of this action by establishing communications and coordination with those who will be affected?*

No. I didn't even talk with anyone about it.

3. *Is the implementation method I have chosen the result of a thoughtful situation analysis, including "best" and "worst" case anticipated results, or am I following normal practices?*

There wasn't time to do all of that. The mission had to be accomplished right now regardless of the immediate results. Perhaps we can fix it later.

What this person needed was an understanding of the attitude of cost elimination. He forgot all about people being more important than things or people needing to participate in actions. Consider cost elimination as an attitude that can be developed.

If your company is making 5 percent after taxes, you must have a $20 increase in sales in order to show a $1 increase in net profit. If you can determine a way not to spend $2, without hurting the operation, you will achieve the same result.

The problem, of course, is to determine which $2 not to spend. You do not want to reduce your capability of properly managing the business or cause your people to become so confined in their thinking that they miss opportunities.

Anyone can reduce costs. A few strokes of the pen and the sales department is eliminated, or the factory is subleased, or clerks are rationed on a per-square-foot basis. Nothing to it.

Unfortunately, much cost elimination is accomplished in just such an emotional or sporadic way. We all know of companies that initiate huge layoffs only to find, in a little while, that they must rehire and retrain.

Cost elimination is an attitude, and one that can be learned.

The sense of cost elimination is this: Managers are career trained and job oriented to a growing operation and a growing economy. When his company and/or the economy gets in trouble, the manager must shift from this conventional style and enter the foreign world of doing things more cheaply. To him, cost elimination is a random thing forced by an oppressive environment, rather than a creative function exercised as part of a management concept.

This is always painful, undignified, and traumatic. No one ever forgets his personal experience in such an event. Constructive programs have to be junked. Valuable personnel must be eliminated. The whole operation is deliberately cut back knowing that the road to recovery may be a long one. Top executives mutter about overexpansion, collapsing markets, and perhaps federal control. There is confusion in the executive ranks.

The facts of life are that the company did not keep cost elimination as a basic part of its management program. Suggestion programs, value analysis efforts, work effectiveness and the like are assuredly conducted as a routine part of doing business. However, the overexpansion, the overorganization, and the neglect of expenses did not originate with the people who contribute to those functions.

Cost elimination as a critical action only comes about because it has been neglected as a continuing necessity. We get fat because we lose sight of our purpose and control. What exists has been done to us by ourselves.

To remedy this, it is necessary to approach cost elimination in an entirely different manner. It must be a constant function by which managers' performance is measured. It must contain innovation and creativity and it must be equitably administered.

Present cost-elimination programs can fail because they are dull and painful. Honest managers find themselves faced with the same across-the-board cuts that the more experienced budget padders can easily survive. Each cost revolution exposes the fact that the management does not have a consistent attitude of cost elimination.

While concern for cost is a primary factor in management, this concern is sometimes clouded by difficulty in recognizing opportunities for improvement. We get to know so much about our business that we lose the capacity to view it objectively. We may feel that what already surrounds us must always be; and worse, we may decide that we already are as cost conscious as it is possible to be.

Take the matter of travel. Many companies insist that their executives travel tourist class in order to save the additional 10 percent fare. Nobody who flies regularly likes the uncomfortable seats, the hurried service, and the overall humiliation that accompanies tourist. When the victim arrives at his destination he is usually disgruntled, and he certainly is not in a company mood.

However, if you challenge a man to provide cost-elimination suggestions equivalent to 20 percent of his air fare over the year, with the provision that he will fly first class anyway, you will come out ahead. That will give him something to think about on the plane. If he is a staff troubleshooter type, challenge him to pick up a cost elimination, on each trip, equivalent to the total price of his expenses, in addition to his regular task. He'll love it. . . .

Why be interested in cost elimination?

If you aren't, who will be?

The history of most companies shows a pattern of growth followed by slowing followed by growth and so on through the generations. What isn't shown so clearly is that interest in cost elimination is inversely proportional to the position of the cycle the company is enjoying. When everything is going great, expansion and risk are the buzz words. With the first recognizable sign of let down—the axe starts swinging. Cost-reduction objectives are immediately established, and grim faced executives tearfully tear the operation apart to reach those goals. This traumatic experience creates such an internal disturbance that the company may feel an additional self-produced reduction cycle before recovering. At any rate, the survivors will never look at the company or its management in the same way as before. I don't need to be too explicit—we have all been through it.

But if the managers are cost-elimination conscious at all times, the company will never get fat. The problem is to make this attitude happen during times of plenty, so that you never get caught with your costs up.

Thus cost elimination must be a continuous and personal program that is never neglected for more attractive and temporary pursuits.

What causes unnecessary cost increases?

Consider this question in the reverse. What do you do when costs must be cut dramatically? You chop up the organization; condense the jobs to be done; eliminate people; wipe out branch offices; and, in general, pull everything together into a tighter, more cost conscious environment. This must mean that you got a little carried away in the first place.

This thought applies to a total company problem. Most of us aren't concerned with that. But if you think of it on the basis of a department operation, or even a group, the pattern is the same. When reduction time comes, we suddenly find that we have been oriented toward unending growth. Our personnel discussions have been concerned only with development and promotion.

Cost acceleration is also an attitude.

But the basic thing that causes costs to increase is lack of attention to their growth. As an earnest but inadequate golfer, I can state factually that almost all the trouble in my game stems from removal of the eye from over the ball. Knowing this does not automatically eliminate it. Systematical discipline is involved and required. Those who can enforce self-discipline are successful. Those who don't, never get to cash their stock options.

What is the difference between prevention, elimination, and reduction?

Cost prevention is a result of evaluating something so thoroughly prior to getting involved that you don't spend the money unless the result is sure to be profitable. Sometimes managers play games with this category by saying things like: "I decided not to paint the factory, and so I'm putting in a savings of $56,000." "I didn't buy that Rolls." This usually comes under the heading of cost avoidance.

Cost prevention is a continuing evaluation of new projects, hiring, organization expansion, and similar routine exercises in a manner that makes them prove their own worth. It is obvious to everyone that hiring $100,000 worth of salesmen to produce $90,000 worth of sales may not be worthwhile in the long run. But it may not be so obvious that reorganizing to create three new department heads may only result in the elimination of at least three people from the work pool while creating a source of no profit-making overhead.

Cost Elimination

To eliminate is to get rid of for good. Take the matter of a product that loses money. It is inevitable that many people will point out that this product is required in order to complete the line, or satisfy special customers, or some other very good reasons. You already know all of them.

However, looked at in the cold light of day, the product is a loser. Only three possible steps exist: Raise the price so that you can make a proper margin, cost reduce it for the same reason, or get rid of it.

Usually the cost reduction (and I'm getting ahead of myself) isn't going to work on this product, and so you should do the other things. If you really need it, have your competitor make it for you and let him lose the money.

Cost elimination is based on the thought of: *Do we need it at all?* rather than: Can we become more efficient or is this the best approach? Much has been written about functions that were established for very good reasons and then outlived their usefulness. I'm sure that somewhere in the federal government, there is still a bureau of stagecoach regulation.

I recommend that you provide each of your key managers with a handsomely mounted bullet suitable for biting. This will serve as a reminder, and you can check their cost-elimination effectiveness by walking around now and then checking for teeth marks.

Cost Reduction

This is like a diet. And like diets, cost reduction is usually accomplished on a crash basis. The success or failure of the project is measured by attaining the lower weight, or expense, set as the target. Like a diet, it is uncomfortable, unnatural, and usually temporary. Your doctor will tell you to lose 15 pounds, but you have no control over which 15 will disappear.

The most effective cost-reduction methods are those approached in a deliberate manner. Value analysis is a practical technique for those who will take the time to understand it. It also generates an attitude, but it is an attitude of improving what you already have. Therefore, apply the elimination test first, and you may save yourself some trouble.

The key to cost reduction is establishing measurable goals and monitoring the progress toward them during the length of the program. But, the goals must be specific. The absolutely worst one you can select is an across-the-board cut of some sort. It is unfair, impractical, and generally ineffective. You will get the reduction, but most of your time will be spent in granting exemptions.

Can you establish cost elimination as a continuing attitude?

Certainly. It is well known that people concentrate on the things they think are important to their leaders. If cost prevention is a sometime thing with them, it is because they feel that it is a sometime thing with top management. They need constant reminders.

There is no reward for being frugal in a growing operation. There is no recognition of proper budget administration. There is no incentive to spend the money properly. Now be honest about the thing. Is there really any value within your area or responsibility for running a tight ship? Think about the people who work for you. If they live within their budget, do you ever mention it?

To make intelligent people cost-elimination conscious, you have to help them recognize that it is an important part of their job. Important to you, and important to their superiors. Of course, if you're going to say it is important, you really have to believe it is. You can't fake it.

If neglect is the primary contributor to increased cost, the lack of imaginative approaches to cost elimination must certainly be an equal factor. Frankly, cost reduction isn't any fun, and cost prevention is looked upon as a personal affront by most people.

I don't know that the whole thing has to be enjoyable, but I do know that people do unpleasant things very poorly. The negative reaction to "cut the cost" orders at every level occur because it is usually an unexpected and abrupt event. Urgency is everywhere. The dollar is the only important thing. Pet projects, boondoggles, and well-formulated plans all meet the same fate.

One attractive and inexpensive way of keeping your people cost-reduction oriented is the BAD program. BAD stands for Buck A Day. The idea is to present to all the people the opportunity and motivation to peer into their own personal jobs and come up with cost reductions equal to $250 per year.

Almost any job has at least this amount of cost savings available from it, and people will dig them out willingly when the atmosphere is right. The first BAD program was conducted at ITT. The public relations men took my broadly sketched concept and developed a whole program featuring a cartoon character with a mask. He was the BAD Guy. Then they developed a series of promotional devices playing on the word BAD: BAD is Good; Join the BAD Guys; BAD Makes Cents, etc. A simple suggestion form, BAD Buck, was devised. The program was explained to supervision, and then to the rest of the personnel. Each and every suggestion submitted was recognized by presenting the suggestor with a coffee cup labeled: "I had a BAD Idea," on one side, and "I am an ITT BAD Guy," on the other. That was the extent of the prizes.

In the ITT divisions employing the one month program, more suggestions were received than employees participating. Average implementation cost was less than $1 per employee. Return on investment was better than 100 to 1. And everyone had a good time.

As a more important fallout of the program, internal communications were significantly improved and the regular suggestion program got a big boost. The program is repeated annually, with the same effect.

Guidelines for Browsers

Index